Giving Paws

"Martha L. Thompson's book, *Giving Paws: Having a Service Dog for a Hidden Disability* is a soul-baring, honest, compelling account of living with physical and emotional challenges and how a service animal can literally help someone continue surviving."

—DEAR ABBY

"*Giving Paws* is a gem of a book, as entertaining as it is educational. Readers will fall in love with Henry, a little dog with a big heart—and an important job to do."

—BRENDA SCOTT ROYCE, author of *Monkey Love, Champion's New Shoes* and *Bailey the Wonder Dog*

"Martha Thompson's *Giving Paws* is a powerful, deeply personal journey into a better life beside a service dog for invisible disabilities. Challenged by health, public perception, and a deep sense of ethic about the partnership, Thompson forges a life--and a book--that many readers will find compelling, indeed."

—SUSANNAH CHARLESON, NYT bestselling author of *Scent of the Missing* and *The Possibility Dogs.*

"With compelling honesty about her chronic illnesses, Thompson offers keen insights into the therapeutic relationship with service dogs. She is an engaging guide into the expanding world of animal assisted therapy."

—Jacqueline Sheehan, Ph.D., fiction writer, essayist and psychologist. Author of *Tiger in the House, The Center of the World, Picture This, Now & Then* and *Lost & Found.*

"Everyone knows someone with an invisible illness or disability. Yet too few truly appreciate the difficulties faced by those who suffer—not only from the illness, but from the lack of understanding from those closest to them. *Giving Paws: Having a Service Dog for a Hidden Disability* is a heartfelt and moving story of one woman's journey living with invisible illness and disability. It is a must-read for anyone who wants to better understand the challenges that face a family member, loved one or friend with an invisible disability."

—WAYNE CONNELL, Founder and President, Invisible Disabilities Association

"Martha writes with candor, compassion and love for her animals, especially her Service Dog, Henry. She teaches us the many ways Service Dogs can enrich and enable the lives of people who need them. I learned a LOT!

"This book is for anyone who loves dogs, wants or needs a Service Dog or wants to understand how vital they are to someone with a disability. I thoroughly enjoyed it."

—PAM WRIGHT, 25 year Docent for the Greater Los Angeles Zoo Association

"This memoir is a testament to strength of the bond between dogs and humans, and to the resiliency of our relationships with them. Service dogs, no matter what their size or breed, provide beacons of hope, comfort and vital assistance to those who rely on them. As is told in this moving story, little Henry turned out to be the ideal co-pilot for his person, Martha."

—CLAUDIA KAWCZYNSKA, *The Bark* | Editor-in-Chief

"When I read Martha Thompson's first draft of *Giving Paws* more than three years ago, I knew this work had the potential to become a published memoir. Thompson became a professional writer during the process, learning the difficult task of editing and rewriting her own work. The final product is compelling, harrowing and heartwarming. It is a confession, an entertainment and gentle advocacy for those who can benefit from having service animals in their lives, for differing health reasons. Based on other work I've seen from Thompson, I know she has many more stories to tell. Keep your eye on this writer."

—STEVEN STIEFEL, writer and memoir editor, Co-writer of *Making Rumours*, with Ken Caillat, the album's producer.

Giving Paws:
Having a Service Dog for a Hidden Disability

by Martha L. Thompson

ISBN 978-1-63393-499-3

Published by

◤ köehlerbooks™

210 60th Street
Virginia Beach, VA 23451
800-435-4811
www.koehlerbooks.com

Giving Paws

*Having a Service Dog
for a Hidden Disability*

Martha L. Thompson

VIRGINIA BEACH
CAPE CHARLES

For my husband Don

Table of Contents

Introduction

WHEN I REACHED MY FORTIES, I was pretty healthy, which was surprising because I'd been battling the demons of anorexia nervosa since adolescence, and a primary immunodeficiency disease since my mid-thirties. This disease, Common Variable Immune Deficiency, or CVID, was anything but common. It caused me to have collagenous colitis, a fancy name for daily diarrhea, and coccidioidomycosis, or valley fever, which destroyed my left lung. The lung was removed and I started getting monthly infusions of immunoglobulin. Supposedly, this would keep me from getting any more life-threatening infections.

In the ten years that followed my CVID diagnosis, I had fewer horrible infections, but continued my mad dashes to the bathroom, which triggered dizzy spells and frequent fainting. My internist referred me to a cardiologist who ran a lot of tests and found that I had low blood pressure and a thickened heart valve. He wasn't terribly worried, and suspected my fainting was due to dehydration and malnutrition. I thought he'd send me back to the gastroenterologist, but he had something else in mind. He suggested I get a service dog.

I'd heard that dogs could be trained to assist people with both physical and psychiatric illnesses, but the idea of getting one hadn't occurred to me. Were my illnesses serious enough to warrant a service dog? According to my doctor and the Americans with Disabilities Act, they were. With the hope of restoring some normality to my life, I took my doctor's advice.

I adopted an irresistible, black and tan dachshund/chihuahua puppy and named him Henry. For nine months, we went to class and practiced diligently. He learned specific tasks to assist me, and I learned how to communicate with him. As a team, we were tested by an experienced service dog trainer and Henry started coming with me to work. Naïvely, I believed his support would magically restore my health and make life easier. I was wrong.

During the first week of having Henry with me in my office at the zoo, his presence drew so much attention to me and my "disability," I wanted to crawl under my desk and hide. Complete strangers asked, "What's wrong with you?" I got so embarrassed about being ill, I wanted to abandon the whole idea and just let Henry be a pet.

When a person with a service dog has an obvious disability like blindness, no one asks questions or passes judgment, but when people looked at me they saw a skinny person with a little dog, and wondered what my problem was. They wanted to know *why* I needed him. Telling complete strangers about my compromised immune system and anorexia was humiliating. Even after I answered their questions, many still didn't understand. Henry's Tom Thumb stature and disarming dog appeal fueled their curiosity, causing them to stare and ask, "He's so little. How does he help you?" At the time, I wished I had chosen a big ugly dog so onlookers would have left us alone.

I loved little Henry, but his presence was making my life harder, not better. I wanted to give up and let him retire, but fortunately, Henry wasn't ready for that. He did his job and stuck with me as I learned to negotiate life with a service dog.

CHAPTER 1

Gus

DOGS INSTINCTIVELY RESPOND WHEN their owners show signs of distress. They want to be near you when you're sick in bed, and can lift your spirits if you're feeling blue. My experience with the healing ability of dogs started with a special German shepherd mix named Gus, who was not a trained service dog, but intuitively supported me when I needed him.

Gus came into my life when I was a thirty-one-year-old actor living in a one-bedroom apartment on Central Park West Avenue and 103rd street in Manhattan in 1991. This put me just a few blocks south of Harlem, across from the unpopulated, junkie-ridden northern part of the famous park, and half a block east of a huge, crime-infested cluster of housing projects. My apartment was on the second floor of a four-story building that faced 103rd street, directly above a subway station. This meant I could feel and hear people coming and going into the hole in the ground at all hours of the day and night. The pulse of the neighborhood was unsettling.

Prior to moving to 103rd street, I'd thought I was pretty tough, because I'd lived in Manhattan before. I'd also lived in Queens, Jersey City and Brooklyn during my college and graduate school years. Now I wanted so badly to be back in Manhattan that I was willing to take the risk of living in a dicey area. However, during my first week as a resident on CPW Ave, I heard gunshots on four consecutive nights, probably triggered by activity in one of the crack houses adjacent to my building. My thick skin thinned. Every night I feared that someone was going to break into my apartment.

As scared as I was, I didn't want a roommate, but I didn't want to be alone either. One night, while I was lying in bed trembling, listening to the angry voices on the street, a solution flashed into my head like a bolt of lightning. What if I got a dog?! I'd wanted one of my own since I was a kid, but as an adult living in New York I had been so consumed by school—first four years at Marymount Manhattan College, then four at the Juilliard School—that there would have been no way I would have had time to properly care for one. But now, I spent my time auditioning and sometimes working, so having a dog was totally realistic. In fact, it was a brilliant idea! I'd have protection and companionship. All I needed was to find the right furry, four-footed friend.

The next morning, I called the ASPCA, which was just across town on East 96th Street. Even though the idea had come from my fear, the dream of owning my own dog ignited an untapped tenderness in me. Thinking about taking care of another living being sparked a feeling I'd never had before: a combination of a powerful mothering instinct and infatuation. A door in my heart opened to a new kind of happiness.

At four o'clock on a Friday afternoon, I finished my shift selling perfume at Bloomingdale's 59th Street, my day job at the time, hurried onto the subway, rode to 96th Street, and bounced into the ASPCA, eager to find a canine friend. My impulsive energy was squelched when the man at the front desk explained that I had to fill out numerous forms, provide personal and professional references, and prove that I had a job and a telephone in my name. In other words, I had to pass their inspection as a caretaker. This policy prevented animals from going to homes that could not afford or support them. Pen in hand, I carefully filled out all the forms.

After an hour, I presented my completed forms to the man at the front desk, and he made phone calls to verify my place of employment and phone number. Next, I was escorted by a volunteer kennel attendant, an older African-American man, to a room filled with cages. Incessant barking echoed off the cement walls. The space looked like a locker room and smelled of urine, feces, and doggy body odor. Oddly enough, I found that very comforting. All the innocent, furry prisoners in the cells were calling out, "Pick me! Pick me!"

Slowly walking past the cages, I looked into the eyes of each hopeful orphan. "Take me home!" each of them cried. When I found the root-beer-colored eyes of a German shepherd mix with a handsome widow's peak, I stopped in my tracks. His black ears flopped halfway down atop his cute tan face, making him irresistible.

"Could I get a closer look at this one?" I asked Mr. Volunteer Man.

"Sure. Come on, Big Boy." He entered the cage and put a leash around the dog's neck.

"Is that his name? Big Boy?" I was falling in love.

"I don't know. He was brought in a week ago. Someone found him wandering the streets around Columbia University."

"Poor guy. His owner must miss him. Why haven't they come to get him?"

"No one will come. We get a lot of strays from that area, 'cause students get puppies, then when classes let out, they move and just set the dogs loose on the street."

"Really?" I couldn't believe anyone could be so heartless. Big Boy wagged his tail so hard when I went to pet him, his hips swiveled. His ears went back, and he thrust himself against me, begging for love. He was the one.

"You want 'im?" Mr. Volunteer Man calmly asked.

"I'll have to come back tomorrow. I'm not prepared to take him home tonight. Can I get him tomorrow?" *Please, please, please, don't turn me down.*

"Well, I can't promise he'll still be here, but you can come back. He's already been here six days."

"I promise I'll come back. I promise, Big Boy, I'll be back." In kennel time, six days meant he was on death row. It meant he would soon be put down. The next day was Saturday, and I prayed that they wouldn't destroy him on a Saturday.

As I walked out of the ASPCA, a happy song played in my head, and this dog's beguiling face was taking up residence in my heart. The next day, I would come back for him. Skipping to the subway station, then descending the stairs, the name "Gus" popped into my mind. Gus. My pup's name would be "Gus." In less than twenty-four hours, I hoped, we would be together.

When I returned the next day, I looked for Mr. Volunteer Man, but he was not there. I asked a younger guy if I could get the dog I'd seen the day before. He said he wasn't sure which one I meant, but he'd walk me to the cages and let me have a look. The once-noisy room was now silent, and the cages empty. Where were all the dogs?

"It's Saturday. There were a lot of adoptions today," the young man explained.

"Did they all get adopted?"

"Yeah, probably."

I didn't want to think where the others had gone. Where was my Gus? Had he been put to sleep? Had someone taken him home? The young man disappeared and I stood in the middle of the cold, cement room. Tears came to my eyes. Suddenly, I heard a snort from the far corner cage and I rushed to get a better look. There he was; there was that face. It was Gus! *My* Gus. He'd waited for me. He was the only dog in the room. We were meant to be together. I vowed to care for him for the rest of his life.

My fortuitous, immediate love for Gus opened a door in my heart that would save my life. Discovering that I could love another being was a blessing and a step toward a healthier identity.

Before handing Gus over to me, the shelter attendant was obliged to tell me that they knew nothing about this dog's history and couldn't tell me what to expect of him. No problem.

The moment Gus's leash was in my hand, he took off at full speed. I gripped the leash as tightly as I could. Before I could take a breath, we were flying down the sidewalk. Oh man, Gus was fast and strong! Could I manage him? Was I in over my head?

Gus was just happy to be free. He had a huge smile on his face, and I was sure he knew he'd escaped the dreaded fate of so many pound puppies. My arm muscles would be built up in no time, and we'd be fine. Suddenly I had a very clear goal: I was going to be the best mommy I could be.

The two of us flew joyfully through Central Park en route to my apartment, Gus's new home. As we walked, I told him as much as I could about myself and how our new life together was sure to be grand. As we passed people in the park, I noticed that they were afraid of Gus. Great! With him at my side I wouldn't have to feel so vulnerable when I went for a jog. My Gus would protect me.

Happiness pumped through my heart as I walked Gus home. Our first activity together was taking a bath. He was grimy, covered with fleas, and smelly. Other than that, he was dreamy. Having no experience with bathing dogs, I coaxed him into the tub with a Milk-Bone dog biscuit, which I had optimistically bought the day before, and then lathered him up with Flex shampoo. He was very squirmy, so I got a good workout. Afterward the bathroom was soaked and coated with thick, German shepherd fur.

The minute he sensed that I was finished, he jumped out of the tub and bolted wildly into the living room. He ran in circles, slipping on the wet, wooden floor, then shook his body from head to toe, spraying the walls with furry droplets. Even though we were making a huge mess, I laughed out loud. Trying to stop him was futile, so I sat back and enjoyed his playfulness. When he finally settled down, he snuggled his wet, wooly body next to mine on the couch, and we had a cozy evening together.

The largeness of my new responsibility started sinking in, but I was so relieved to have a companion. I also felt confident that I would be a good dog mommy. Thinking about life with Gus and tending to all his needs would replace the tiresome negative thoughts I had about myself. Looking at his ever-smiling face soothed my soul.

When Gus came into my life, I was suffering from depression, but physically healthy. My weight was low, but in the normal range for a small-boned woman my age. I had no idea what a positive impact he would have on my survival in the coming years. Staying healthy had been critical in order to pursue my dream of being an actor. However, I was constantly at risk of slipping into the clutches of anorexia nervosa, which had been threatening my life since adolescence.

Within six months of adopting Gus, my agent advised me to move to Los Angeles to get some West Coast acting credits on my resume. They said I had significant East coast experience and that going to LA would put some air in the sails of my career. At first this idea repulsed me, because my impression of California actresses was that they were all blond, busty, and beautiful. Where and how would a skinny tomboy like me fit in? My agency explained that their LA office was eager to meet me, and that if I did not go to LA, there was not much more they could do for me in New York.

My love for Gus helped me process my dilemma. Once I started to imagine life in Southern California, I realized that we would no longer have to live in a cement city, or take walks on sidewalks that stank of urine. California had sandy beaches, grassy mountain trails, blue skies, warm weather, houses, and yards. Gus and I could have a better life!

CHAPTER 2

Welcome to Los Angeles

PRIOR TO LEAVING NEW YORK, I sublet my apartment to a friend of a friend named Mitchell. He was so grateful to get an apartment in Manhattan that he gave me the phone number of his ex-boyfriend John, who needed a roommate in Santa Monica. My agent had moved to Santa Monica the year before, so I figured it must be nice. When I looked at the map of Los Angeles that I'd been studying for weeks and saw how close Santa Monica was to the beach, I knew that was where I wanted to live.

"Hi, John," I said, leaving a voicemail. "This is Martha, Mitchell's friend in New York, and he said you were looking for a roommate. I just wanted to find out if it would be okay for me to bring my dog. Please let me know if that's a problem. Thanks. I look forward to hearing from you." In less than an hour he called me back and left this message:

"Hi Martha! This is John. Didn't Mitch tell you? It is a *requirement* that you have a dog! Call me when you can. Ciao." John's West Highland Terrier, Maggie, wanted a friend. He spoke as if we'd been friends for years and as if he were just waiting for Gus and me to move in.

After playing phone tag a couple more times, I finally reached him, and he was even friendlier than his voicemail messages.

"Your rent will be $500 a month, and I won't take a penny more," he joked.

"Really?" It seemed too low.

"Really. So?" He waited for my reply.

"Yes, of course, that's so generous of you. Thanks!"

"Going once . . . going twice . . . sold! So when can we expect you?"

"We'll be there in a month." Gus and I were going to be living in a nice apartment in Santa Monica, just ten minutes from the beach!

After packing up my apartment, Gus and I flew from New York to my mother's house in Wisconsin. Mom very graciously gave me her 1983 Pontiac LE-6000 four-door sedan. She said she and her husband Larry were about to get new cars anyway, so I could have her old one. Wow, my very own car! *My very first* car! My mother was a very generous woman, and her gift was especially dear to me, since there was no way I could afford to buy a car myself.

After spending a few days with Mom and Larry and getting acquainted with my Pontiac, which I named "Lee," Gus and I took off. For the next seven days, Gus marked his territory every few hours as we made our way across the country. Because I was a new driver, I took my time on the road. Gus was the perfect traveling companion, because he never questioned my driving choices and listened to me as I sorted through all my anxiety about moving.

When we arrived in Santa Monica via the 405 Freeway on a beautiful Sunday afternoon in January, we fell in love with the big blue sky and ever-present sun. Maggie and Gus became fast friends, as did John and I. He was kind and sensitive, and most important, he loved dogs.

***

Professionally, I got lucky in my first year in Southern California. I performed in three plays and did guest appearances on a network sitcom and a serial drama. The most surprising job I got was a national commercial for a major beer that aired frequently from Thanksgiving Day through the Super Bowl. It paid the bills for a while, and it was fun to brag about, but it was not very satisfying artistically.

The actual job only lasted three days, most of which were spent sitting around on a fancy-pants ranch in Camarillo, waiting to shoot my scenes. For sixty very lucrative seconds, I played a farmer's wife sitting at a holiday meal with a large, goofy, animated turkey that had come as a dinner guest. The experience was fun, but I yearned for projects that would provide an artistic community and would last longer than three days.

After all my apprehension about moving to Los Angeles, I was thrilled to discover how much I loved about it. Being able to drive around in my own car and come and go as I pleased was so refreshing. It sure beat having to depend on the smelly, crowded subway trains. The whole time I had been living in New York, I was so mesmerized by the pulse of the city that I never really missed the safe, clean streets I'd grown up on. But as I settled into my new life in Santa Monica, I remembered how much I appreciated them.

Gus seemed to like Southern California as much as I did. He had a yard to play in and could be outside as quickly as I could open the back door. Naïvely, I thought the new happiness Gus and I found in Southern California was going to last forever.

But within my first year of living in California, three of my family members passed away: first Larry, then both of my mother's parents. Of course, this was much more devastating for my mother than for me, but it struck fear in my heart about losing my parents. How does one prepare for that?

Before my fear and sadness could do any damage, I had an encounter on a plane that changed the trajectory of my life. Returning to Los Angeles from Indiana, where I had attended my grandfather's funeral, I found myself in the Boon, Kentucky airport for a forty-five-minute layover. To pass the time I buried my head in a television script I hoped to be working on soon. When the announcement came for everyone to board the plane, I found my seat and plunked myself down. Sitting to my right was a nice-looking man with a boyish smile. We exchanged pleasantries, and I promptly fell asleep.

Half an hour later I woke up drooling. As I wiped the slobber from my chin I laughed at myself. The man with the boyish smile laughed with me.

"How was your nap?" he asked.

"Great. Sorry about the drool."

"It happens to the best of us." He was kind. At that moment, I saw a book in his hand.

"What are you reading?" I asked trying to divert the focus from my slobbery face.

"*The Tibetan Book of Living and Dying,*" he said.

"Sounds good." It really did sound good because I had been thinking so much about death lately. *This guy must be spiritually evolved and smart if he's reading that book. I won't mind sitting next to him for the next three hours.*

"Where are you headed?" he suddenly asked.

"Los Angeles. Santa Monica really. How about you?"

"Silverlake," he said. Although I'd never actually been there, I'd seen it in the old Thomas Guide my roommate had given me and knew it was within Los Angeles city limits. *I wonder what this guy's story is. He's pretty nice.*

"My name is Martha, by the way."

"Nice to meet you, 'Martha By The Way.' I'm Don." *And he has a good sense of humor too. He's way too smart and funny to be single.*

"Do you have kids?" I had to ask, but it sounded so abrupt when it came out.

"No, not married. How about you?"

"No, neither." *What a relief. What about a girlfriend?*

"Are you seeing anyone?" he asked.

"Nothing serious," I said. "How about you?" *Please, please, please say "no."*

"Not right now," he answered. *Now what do I say?*

"May I get either of you a drink?" The flight attendant magically appeared, filling the awkward moment.

"Sure, I'll have a Diet Coke, please," I said.

"And I'd like some water."

"So, what kind of work do you do?" I asked, wanting to know more about this guy who seemed too good to be true.

"A couple of things."

"Like what?"

"I judge scripts for the Academy of Motion Pictures," he said without bragging.

"That's cool. I'm an actor," I said, pointing out that we had something in common.

"I see that you're reading a script."

"Yeah, I have an audition for an episode of *Diagnosis Murder*. Maybe I'll get to work with Dick Van Dyke."

"What kinds of things have you done?"

"Mostly theatre in New York. I went to the Juilliard School," I said, trying not to boast. I wanted him to understand I was serious about acting.

"Juilliard, huh?" I was relieved he knew what it was. "I studied filmmaking at the University of Texas in Austin and directed a few films, but haven't been doing that much lately. These days I split my time between the Academy and Major League Baseball. One of my other jobs is charting pitches during games at Dodger Stadium for a company called STATS. Do you like sports?"

"I like baseball because I played it as a kid. I tried to get on the Little League team when I was eleven, but in 1973, they didn't allow girls on the team. They told me to try out for the boys' soccer team. So I did, and they took me, but I was the only girl and we lost every game. But it was fun because all the boys' moms cheered for me."

During what felt like our first date on the plane, complete with dinner and a movie, Don's smiling, blue eyes and witty conversation had me laughing at a time when I least expected it.

When the plane landed in Los Angeles, we got off and walked together toward baggage claim. *How do I say goodbye? Is he going to ask me out? Maybe I should ask him. How do I do that?*

"Do you want to go for coffee sometime?" he asked, averting his eyes and bowing his head.

"Yeah, that would be great," I said.

"May I have your phone number?" he asked politely.

"Yes, of course." I rifled through my backpack for a piece of paper and a pen and wrote my number down. "It was nice to meet you, Don."

"Likewise, I'm sure, Martha By The Way." He spotted his friend who was picking him up and waved goodbye. Somehow in my state of bliss, I made it to the baggage claim area and found my suitcase. The darkness that had been consuming my energy for the past few weeks lifted and was replaced by a childlike excitement about my new smiley-faced friend, Don.

Meeting Don was no accident. That night on the plane, our destinies merged. Coincidently, a preacher man had been sitting across the aisle from us on the plane, whose presence, I'm sure, blessed our union. Our timing could not have been better.

A few days passed before Don called, and again, the timing felt right. He came to Santa Monica and took me out to lunch, which turned into an evening at the movies. We saw *The Last Seduction,* a neo-noir thriller that was playing in a little theatre near my apartment. In our discussion afterward at a coffee shop, I learned how knowledgeable Don was about filmmaking. Going to movies together was something we both enjoyed and it became a regular activity for us.

We shared meals and conversations, went on hikes and visited museums. Our bond strengthened daily, and it was clear that we were meant to be together; like two trees whose branches intertwine as they grow next to each other.

From the very start, I knew that Don was one of a kind. His genuine jaunty demeanor lifted my spirits, and his clever wit, though sometimes biting, could trigger uncontrollable laughter.

He was unlike anyone I had ever met: childlike and grown-up at the same time, intellectual and goofy, often respectfully careful but sometimes guilelessly frank about his feelings. He was honest to a fault, occasionally brutally so, and would not sugar coat anything to avoid hurt feelings. Unlike me, the people-pleaser, Don was secure with himself and didn't care what others thought of his opinions. At first this intimidated me, but I came to envy his self-confidence and saw him as a role model.

When we met, I was thirty-two and Don was thirty-nine, which was perfect because I needed a partner who had more life experience and wisdom than I had. We had both been in long-term relationships that had lasted more than four years, but I don't think either of us had felt as comfortable with another person as we did with each other. Our being together felt right from the moment we met. Love at first sight? You bet.

From our first conversation on the plane, Don's intellect excited me. Like my dad, he'd studied history in college, and because that was an aspect of Dad that I thought of fondly, I was comforted by Don's knowledge. As a student of filmmaking, his artistic eye was sharp. He saw films and plays from a director's perspective, meaning he saw the big picture. I, on the other hand, saw everything from an actor's point of view and experienced the character's emotional arc. In this way we were different, but we could still communicate about many aspects of creative expression, whether it was films, plays, television shows, or books.

One big difference between us was that Don knew how to take care of himself, and I did not. As the child of an abusive, alcoholic father, he learned how to detach from the drama and get his own needs met. Somehow, my emotional wiring got tangled during childhood and the coping skills I developed were damaging to my body and mind. Instead of detaching and taking care of myself under duress, I withdrew and shut down. This was most problematic during my adolescent years, when I was contending with anorexia. Thankfully, when I was fifteen, I could turn my thinking around enough to gain some weight, graduate from high school, and go on to college and graduate school.

When I met Don, I was maintaining a healthy weight because working as an actor required that I look good. But I was not entirely free from self-destructive thinking. Of course, Don noticed that I didn't eat very much and that my meals were very methodical and repetitious. I wasn't in the habit of talking about my anorexia because I wanted to leave it in the past, but as Don and I got closer, I felt he should know. I trusted him with my feelings, but wasn't sure how he'd respond. When I told him, he didn't look surprised, and I could see by the kindness in his eyes that he was not judging me.

After I divulged my childhood challenges, Don told me about his. He explained that once he had fled from his violent father and victimized mother, he'd gone to State College in Pennsylvania, following in the footsteps of his half-brother Craig, eight years his senior. He often used the word "escape" to describe that departure. Having been in the accelerated classes throughout junior high and high school, he knew he could use his intellect to open up doors to a better world.

His upbringing was not all torment. In fact, he had a deep fondness for his mother, who lived and breathed for her two sons. When Don first spoke about her, he did so with compassion, and revealed that as a child he had to physically defend her, once with a baseball bat, from his violent dad. His love for his defenseless mother showed me a sensitivity that allowed me to trust him. Her doting nurturance had taught him how to love.

Don's ability to love me was important, but I needed him to love Gus as well. The first time he came to the apartment I shared with my friend John and his little dog, Maggie, I introduced him to Gus and tried to impress upon him that Gus was as precious to me as a firstborn child. Don had never said anything that suggested he didn't like dogs, but when he met Gus his shoulders tensed up, and he took a step back.

"He won't bite you," I said as Gus playfully approached him, wiggling his butt, hoping to be scratched. Gus was a friendly dog and had never shown aggressive behavior toward any of my friends.

"Have you ever had a dog?" I asked.

"As a kid, my mom had a cocker spaniel named Inky, but that was a long time ago."

"Do you like dogs?" I figured I had better ask up front, since I knew it would be hard for me to hang out with someone who didn't like them.

"Yeah, I just haven't been around them much." Gus took this opportunity to lean into Don's legs, which told me he approved of Don. "Hey, buddy," Don said and reached down to give him a good scratch at the base of his tail.

"Gus likes you," I said, not surprised, but definitely pleased. "You found his sweet spot."

"That's good, because I can see who 'Number One' is around here." Don was right. Gus was my 'Number One.'

"You know what they say? 'Love me, love my dog.'" I joked, and yet I was completely serious. "Did you know that expression came from a French monk named Saint Bernard of Clairvaux around 1100 AD? Actually, he used it in a sermon and said it was from an old proverb." Since Don had studied history in college, I hoped he'd appreciate my historical trivia.

Don had a cat named Hollingsworth, whom I looked forward

to meeting. The only cat I'd ever lived with was a gigantic black cat named Midnight, who really belonged to my big sister Rachel. She got him when I was born, and he lived to be fourteen. He was a wonderful addition to my childhood. So even though I had not lived with a cat since I was a kid, I liked them well enough. My fondness for Don made me more willing to love his cat, and I hoped he would feel the same about Gus.

Before meeting Don, I had been fiercely independent. My mother had demonstrated that it was possible to work, manage all the financial affairs, and raise four kids without a husband. She divorced my dad when I was six, and then did an amazing job of being the breadwinner and head of the household. By example, she taught me to be independent. So when I started dating, it never occurred to me to look for someone who would provide for me. A big part of it was that I didn't want anyone controlling my comings and goings. However, when I entered my early thirties and self-doubt started creeping in, the idea of someone sweeping me off my feet and fathering me started to sound good. I kept these thoughts to myself, though, because I was afraid to appear needy or weak.

One evening, when Don and I were having dinner in a Thai restaurant near his apartment, we started talking about our prior relationships. Since our feelings for each other were solid, it wasn't threatening or weird to hear about previous girlfriends and boyfriends. The guy I had been seeing when I met Don had been so wrong for me that I had to laugh about it. He was a neurologist whom I'd met in a coffee shop in Santa Monica. His name was Jeff, and he told me he liked to play guitar, which appealed to my creative side, but after I got to know him a little, it was very clear that he wanted to have total control over my life. He even spoke about marriage, but it came with the condition that I stop acting and let him be the breadwinner. The needy child inside me liked that, but the independent adult felt smothered. We only dated for three months.

When I shared with Don how Jeff needed to be the provider or father figure, Don abruptly said, "Don't expect me to father you. I'm not going to father anyone." His tone was so defensive, it startled me. Did he think I was looking for someone to take care of me? Did I seem needy? How embarrassing. Where was my stubborn independence? Was I losing it? Fortunately, our dinner conversation got interrupted by the waiter and we changed the subject.

In our first year together I focused most of my attention on Don and our thriving relationship. We had a good thing going and I wanted to nurture it, which loosened the obsessive grip I had on my pursuit of acting. For the first time in my life I was more interested in a person than my acting career. Although I was having just enough success to keep me involved, my gratification waned. Casting agents encouraged me, but my success wasn't rewarding. Learning to love Don was much more gratifying.

CHAPTER 3

Building
Our Family

IN 1995, ONE YEAR AFTER we met, Don and I rented a house together in Echo Park, near Dodger Stadium. It was a three-bedroom craftsman, built in 1914. The surrounding area was crummy, but we were at the top of a hill, so I didn't feel immersed in the sadness of the run-down little houses on East Sunset Boulevard. Neither of us had any money, but Don knew the landlord, and he gave us a good deal on this wonderful old house. Our living together evolved so organically that I wasn't worried about how we would adjust to each other's rhythms and routines. But there was one thing I was worried about.

"I'm going to let Gus sniff around for a bit so he can get acquainted with all the new smells," I said to Don once we got all our furniture moved in.

"Sounds good. For now, I'll keep Hollingsworth in his crate. He's freaked out."

"How should we introduce them?"

"Once Gus settles down, I'll take Hollingsworth out of the crate and hold him." Gus ran up and down the stairs, and went into each room, sniffing every corner. Once he finished exploring and calmed down, it seemed like a good time to introduce him to Don's cat.

"He's pretty much made the rounds. Shall we see what happens?" I asked, hoping Gus wouldn't kill Hollingsworth.

"Let's do it." With that, Don poured Hollingsworth onto the couch. In a heartbeat, Gus darted toward him and the cat bolted. There was such a flurry of activity I didn't see where Hollingsworth went.

"Where is he?" I asked, following Don into the kitchen in the back of the house.

"He's on top of the fridge," Don said, laughing.

"That's one place Gus can't reach. Is he okay?"

"I think so."

"I'm sorry my dog wants to kill your cat," I said as I put my arm around Don's waist.

"We'll deal with it," he said without sounding angry. "Maybe the top of the fridge is the perfect place for him. During the day, he'll want to go outside, so he'll really just be up there at night." Even though Don didn't sound mad, I felt guilty.

"At least we know now how Gus feels about cats."

Hollingsworth seemed content with his new living situation, and over the next year, my guilt dissipated. We all settled nicely into our big, old Craftsman home in Echo Park. Our new neighborhood was generally peaceful, and Gus and I enjoyed long walks together in Elysian Park, which was less than half a mile away. As we walked every morning, I started to notice how many stray dogs and cats there were wandering the streets.

One Saturday afternoon, a couple of months after we moved to Echo Park, I saw some movement in the ivy that covered our little front yard. I stepped out onto the porch and saw a strawberry blond dog that looked part chow chow, part samoyed. Gus ran out to greet our visitor and I could see it was a friendly dog. I got closer to look for a collar and learned that this pretty dog was a girl. She looked like a teddy bear and my heart melted. She was not wearing a collar, but she didn't look feral as so many other neighborhood strays did. Had she run away from home? After letting me pet her long, soft fur she laid down on my feet. My heart dictated my actions, and I didn't think twice about welcoming this cuddly canine into our pack. However, because she was so amiable and looked well cared for, I feared that she may have wandered away from her home. In an effort to be a responsible adult, I took her to the nearest city animal shelter, so her original owners would have a chance to find her.

For the next week, I woke up early every morning and went to visit her in the gloomy shelter, secretly hoping that no one would come to claim her. When no one came after seven days, I was thrilled, because it meant we could adopt her. I paid the adoption fee and took her to the vet to be spayed. Because her long fur was exceptionally soft, I named her Ipek, the Turkish word for silk. She quickly got the nickname "Peepers" because she liked to peep over the edge of couches and chairs to see what we were up to.

Gus and Peepers got along well. Gus never really had any enemies, and all Peepers cared about was being with us. Living with two dogs and a cat felt good because it gave us the sense of being a family. For the next year we all lived very happily, but the universe had something more in mind for us.

In January of the following year, I started seeing a scabby, weatherworn dog roaming around at the bottom of our hill on Sunset Boulevard. His caramel-colored fur was grimy and patchy, and his skinny body and face were covered with bite marks and scratches, some of which were fresh with blood. He was shaped like a dingo, with a small waist and big pointy ears, but he was probably a mix of the typical neighborhood stray: pit bull, German shepherd, and chow chow.

When this ghostlike dog appeared in our neighborhood, I usually saw him in the morning, then again after dark, curled up on a small patch of brown grass outside the ramshackle car wash at the bottom of the hill. When he got up from the grass, he walked tentatively, as if he was afraid something awful was about to happen. His innocent but serious face prompted me to slow down and look closer every time I saw him.

After a few days of seeing him curled up near the sidewalk, shivering in the cold January air, I parked my car and got out to say hello. He cowered when I slowly approached him, as if he expected to be hit. His hardened street-dog appearance was misleading because one look into his yellow eyes told me he wanted to be loved. Had anyone ever cuddled this guy?

When I got close enough to pet him, he flinched. Up close, I could see how sparse his fur was. His skin had turned black where the fur had fallen out, which made him look as if he had big, bad acne scars. This meek, skittish dog was obviously the victim of other feral dogs and abusive people. His haggard condition was so bad I started to cry. How could I help him?

Every morning and evening for three weeks, I filled two yogurt containers, one with dog kibble, the other with water, and walked down to the bottom of the hill to offer him nourishment and tenderness. He really needed medical care too.

When I asked the workers at the local car wash if they knew anything about him, they said they had been feeding him rice and beans and called him "Solovino," which meant "He came alone." Their concern for him surprised me. One guy said he'd tried to take him home to give him a bath, but Solovino had barked and whined so much in their backyard that they had to set him free. Visions of him perishing on that grass patch haunted me. So one day I coaxed him with a dog biscuit into the back seat of my car and drove him to the vet for vaccinations and a special bath to treat his skin condition, which turned out to be mange.

On our front porch, I set up a little area for him, complete with blankets, towels, and a teddy bear. Twice a day I put out food and water, hoping he would want to live with us.

One morning, Solovino was crying on the porch. I went out, sat down slowly—hoping he wouldn't wince—put my arms around his mangy neck, and hugged him.

"I love you, buddy. What are we going to do?" Even if the medicated baths cleared up his scabby skin, he wouldn't be adoptable because he looked so rough. In a shelter, he'd be euthanized within a week.

Looking into his contemplative, maize-colored eyes, the name Arty popped into my head. "Solovino" was a sad, lonely name and too hard to say, so I called him Arty.

"What are we going to do, Arty?" I asked again, hoping he'd reply. If I didn't bring him in the house, he'd drift off and die on the street.

Caring for needy dogs made me feel useful. I knew Arty was going to be a lot more work than Peepers, because he was sick and feral, but I was willing to do whatever it took. He was very bashful, so I didn't insist that he come into the house right away, but I let him set up permanent residence in my heart.

Twice a day I gave him worm medicine, and when he showed up for meals, I tried to pet him and brush him so he'd know he was loved and had a home. His sad eyes begged for love and affection, but every time I touched him, even very gently, he jumped. I learned to show him my hands before making contact. He lived outside for a few more days, then finally came in the house. When he wanted to gallivant around the neighborhood, I let him out because I trusted that he'd come back.

Very gradually, Arty learned to trust us and felt comfortable living inside. We became a pack of six. The love my animals gave infused me with confidence like nothing else in my life.

CHAPTER 4

Blindsided

LIFE WAS GOOD FOR the next couple of years. Then one morning the phone started ringing at 7:30 a.m. Thinking it was a wrong number, I returned to my fetal position next to Don in our big, warm bed. *The answering machine can get the call,* I told myself, and started to drift back to sleep, but it rang again. Maybe it was Walter, the director of the film I was scheduled to start the next day? Once I started thinking about the film, I was awake and figured I might as well get up. I put on a shirt and sweat pants and went downstairs to listen to the messages.

When I pushed the play button, I was surprised to hear my big sister Rachel's voice. The serious tone of her message cleared my head. She wanted me to call her back immediately. Now I was scared. Before I could find her phone number, the phone rang a third time. Rachel again. Through choked tears she told me that our father had died in a car accident the night before.

The word "no" fell from my mouth, and I lost sensation in my arms and legs. All I could feel was a stabbing pain in my chest. This kind of thing didn't happen in our family. My relatives lived well into their nineties and died from old age, not car accidents.

As I hung up the phone, I was overcome by tears. Sadness flushed through me in uncontrollable waves. Unable to get up from the chair in Don's office where I was slumped, I resigned myself to just staying there. Suddenly I felt a warm furry body leaning against my left leg.

"Aw, hi, Gustopher," I said, reaching down to rub him behind his ears. "Thank you, honey." He stared up at me with his pretty brown eyes. Needing more comfort, I slid off the chair onto the floor and put my arms around Gus's neck. He stayed there as if he was on duty to comfort and love me.

"Sweet, sweet Gus. Thank you, honey. I love you so much." Gus was not sentimental, but he was very loyal. Arty and Peepers followed him in, but they didn't stay. Gus sat on the floor with me until Don came down from the bedroom twenty minutes later.

"What's going on, honey?" he asked, seeing my crumpled body next to Gus.

"That was my sister on the phone. My dad was killed in a car accident last night." I could barely get my words out.

"Aw, sweetie, I'm sorry. Come here." He lifted me up and held me in his arms as I convulsed with tears. He had lost his father the previous year, so he could relate to my grief.

My mind flashed onto Father's Day, just nine days earlier, and I remembered that I had sent Daddy flowers for the first time in my life. In the previous year, I had made two trips to see him, which was monumental since I had only seen him once in the previous twenty years. When my grandmother's health had started to fail in recent years, I had begun to mend our fragmented relationship by going to visit him.

When I visited him a few months earlier, the last thing I said to him before I boarded the plane was, "I love you." In thirty-four years, I had *never* spoken those words to my dad, but they came spilling from my mouth directly from my heart.

"I love you too, dear," he replied and hugged me. I knew he loved me, but before that day, I had no memory of hearing him say it. The warmth of his hug was surprising as well, but I impulsively hugged him back with all my might.

My latent journey toward my melancholy father had just been terminated as a result of his car crashing head-on into a tree on a small country road in southern Indiana. When his drive came to a fatal halt, at around 5:00 p.m., the sun was shining and there were no other cars in sight. He was driving home from the university where he taught history. Rachel told me he was not wearing his seat belt and that the impact of hitting the tree deployed the airbag, which pushed him up and smashed his head into the ceiling of the car. The paramedics rushed him to the nearest hospital where he died a few hours later from massive brain trauma. He was alone when he died. There were no family members nearby, just some doctors and nurses, whom he did not know. When I pictured this scenario, fear of loneliness gripped me.

***

My dad's sudden death hit me like a Mack truck. I never saw it coming. Grieving aggravated my depression, which revived and emboldened my anorexia. Consequently, I lost all interest in feeding myself. Why bother? Every morning I woke up crying, but when Don asked what was wrong, I couldn't identify anything in particular. For months, I stayed in this state of sorrow.

My only comfort came from taking long walks with Gus. Getting my blood flowing and sharing my feelings with him seemed to stimulate happier thoughts. However, any progress I made would be dashed if I saw a dead cat or dog in the road. My mind would plummet into darkness and all I would think about was the physical suffering that animal had gone through before dying. Vivid scenes of the animal getting hit by a car, feeling great pain, pleading for help, and dying all alone on the cold pavement played over and over in my head. The desolation was more than I could bear. The reality that the animal was just a carcass now and no longer felt pain didn't enter my mind. Morbid thoughts gripped me for hours every time I saw roadkill. My worst fear was losing Gus. What would I do without him?

During this dark period, my anorexia told me I would feel better if I ate less and I believed it. When I tried to eat, to keep from passing out, I would get a terrible grinding feeling in my stomach. When I started a cup of yogurt, I'd get halfway through and give the rest to the dogs. Eating was a burden. The less I ate, the less interest I had in taking care of myself or living.

My anorexia started when I was eleven. It was triggered when my family moved from a small town to a slightly larger one. The emotional trauma of transferring from a junior high school where I was a tomboyish leader of the pack to one where I was just some new kid in a group of girly girls was devastating. They didn't appreciate my unique style and I withdrew emotionally and socially.

In the 1970s, there was little understanding of anorexia nervosa. There were no special hospitals or treatment facilities yet. But after a few years of wallowing in my adolescent angst, I could climb out of my self-destructive hole. At fourteen, I woke up and realized that I wanted to live, so I patched together a daily meal plan from *Ladies' Home Journal* and relied on the structure of my school schedule to keep me from slipping back into myself. Time was on my side and I was able, with great determination and effort, to rebuild my young life and enter adulthood, mostly free from the voices of my anorexic demons.

From then on, I could maintain a slender but healthy body and successfully complete college, graduate school, and pursue an acting career. But at thirty-seven, grappling with the sudden death of my father sent me right back into depression and anorexia. I no longer had the gift of youth to pull me out. Once again anorexia dictated my every move and I was no longer the master of my thoughts or feelings. Withholding nourishment from my withering body comforted me. I clung to the childhood demon that was so familiar.

When I grew so weak that walking Gus became impossible, I knew I had passed a point of no return and wouldn't be able to turn things around on my own as I had when I was a teenager. I started seeing a therapist, who immediately referred me to a psychiatrist and an internist. Without hesitation, they recommended that I go to a hospital. Because I was so weak and depressed, I listened and went into a special hospital in Florida for anorexia nervosa. By this time in 2000, there were good treatment options available for people with eating disorders, which was a huge improvement from when I had first gotten sick as a kid in 1973, when there were none. Feeling defeated, once I got to the hospital in Florida I surrendered to my treatment team and followed their orders.

Two weeks into my treatment, I suddenly started having explosive watery diarrhea. The doctors explained that this was not uncommon during the refeeding process of someone who had been starving for so long. They gave me Imodium and antibiotics and continued to slowly increase my food intake.

My plan was to stay thirty days, but after the first couple of weeks, I understood that the only way I was going to recover was if I totally surrendered and stayed as long as possible. Without the presence of doctors, nurses, and therapists twenty-four hours a day, I didn't stand a chance battling my anorexia. I stayed for five months.

The treatment I was receiving included individual and group therapy and my favorite, art therapy, where I made clay action figures of all the members of my family. I believe my most important healing occurred when my mother came to participate in my treatment. One of her friends had a condominium forty-five minutes from the hospital, where she could stay, making it possible for her to come to therapy with me twice a week and visit every evening for six weeks.

On the day she arrived, she was carrying a large shopping bag. After giving me a big hug she reached into the bag, pulled out a small framed photo and handed it to me. It was a black-and-white photo of a beautiful young woman holding a one-year-old infant in her lap. I'd never seen it before, but I recognized the people in the picture as my mother and me. I had no memories of being held by her, but here was proof that she had. Mom reached back into her shopping bag and pulled out Blanky, a nappy pink baby blanket that had been my first and best childhood friend. Tears came to my eyes as I took Blanky into my arms. He knew all my childhood secrets and had been my greatest comfort. Mom knew that even though I was a grown woman now, I needed to be loved like a baby in order to heal.

When Mom came to therapy with me, it was awkward to dig deep into my emotional issues, but it was necessary. She was only twenty-four years old when she'd had me, and I was the last of four, so there was only so much she could do to nurture each of us. It didn't help that my dad was unsupportive, due to his own problems with depression. Somehow my older siblings were able to grow and thrive, but I was needier, and as an adolescent I chose to starve myself to death in order to get the love and attention I wanted from my mother.

My therapist encouraged me to share all my childhood feelings with my mother. Uncovering and admitting the anger I had toward her felt coldhearted, but she assured me that she wanted to hear it. Mom wanted to know how I felt so she could help me. With my therapist's guidance, we learned to communicate more openly, and we eventually poured our hearts out to each other. Mom commended me for my courage in challenging my anorexia and said she was proud of me. Her participation in my treatment made it possible for me to heal. It was hard to say goodbye after six weeks, but Mom and I had gotten much closer, and we both knew I was going to be all right.

My progress was slow but steady, and even though my diarrhea persisted, after five months, I was eating normally again, I had gained seventeen pounds and was ready to be discharged.

During my hospital stay, the doctors dissuaded me from returning to work in the entertainment business because of the stress involved. Their reasoning was sound, and I was afraid of jeopardizing my recent recovery, so I decided to bow out. At first I was relieved to be free from the demands of an acting career, but I soon learned that walking away from something that had defined me for twenty years was easier said than done.

CHAPTER 5

Discovering the Zoo

ONCE I WAS HOME from the hospital, and no longer had my acting career to provide structure and distract me from my demons, the days grew long and dark. Even though it was the middle of summer in Southern California and days were relentlessly sunny, my mood turned gray. I started to resent the sunshine and felt guilty for not appreciating it. When I looked at the bright blue sky and felt the warmth of the sun, I was ashamed of myself. The mean voices in my head got loud. *You don't deserve to live in this paradise. You don't deserve to live at all.*

All the progress I had made in the hospital—quieting my anorexic voices and gaining weight—started to erode. When I woke up in the morning, I had nowhere to go and nothing to do. Don had recently gotten a great full-time job as a statistical analyst for a sports technology and data company, and he was elated, but I couldn't share his joy. When he left for work in the morning, I felt so lost and alone, I was afraid I was going to kill myself before he got home. I wanted to be supportive, but I felt abandoned.

When I was home by myself every day my only comfort came from Gus, Arty, and Peepers. Their everlasting happy faces and in-the-moment approach to life wouldn't let me give up so easily. I started getting up early to take Gus for a walk. Don would walk Peepers and Arty before he left for work and I would walk Gus. He was always game. Walking got my blood flowing and lifted my spirits. The effect Gus's presence had on my mood, even for an hour a day, was significant.

One morning on our walk, an idea came to me. If spending time with our dogs could lift my spirits, maybe finding a way to work around animals all day long could give me a sense of purpose. Memories of the Tennessee Williams play *The Glass Menagerie* came to mind. In the play Laura, the painfully shy, crippled daughter, finds comfort in drifting around the zoo every day instead of attending the business classes her mother has signed her up for. When she is not at the zoo, she withdraws into the fanciful world of her collection of glass animal figurines, which she cares for with great tenderness.

Identifying with Laura came easily to me because, like her, I was attracted to animals, rudderless in life, and prone to living in my imagination. The big difference between us was that I had a lifetime of ambition and achievement behind me, where Laura had been repressed and dominated by her mother her whole life. She was the kind of character I loved to play when I was acting, because I could relate so well to her incapacitating sensitivity, but unlike her, I was not willing to stay stuck in my unhappiness.

Thinking about Laura in *The Glass Menagerie* sparked an idea to explore our local zoo. *Maybe I could get some entry-level, part-time job there.* When I looked in the newspaper want ads I found no leads, but in a local community college catalogue I found a six-week course called "An Introduction to Zoo Operations." What great timing! The class would be starting in July, just a few weeks away.

Before the first class, I went to the zoo to familiarize myself with this promising new world. The day was warm and sunny, just like every other day, but I felt different. My heart was lighter and when the sunshine invited me to enjoy it, I accepted. Mid-week at 11:00 a.m., the zoo parking lot was pretty empty, so I could park close to the entrance. After waiting in line for thirty seconds, I bought my ticket and entered the zoo. Peacefulness came over me as I walked past the gift shops and concession stands in search of some animals. After five minutes of walking, I came upon the first exhibit, the meerkats. Their area was completely open, no bars, no glass. Two of the meerkats stood upright, looking very alert and very cute.

"Hi, guys. How's it going?" I asked, knowing I might sound loony to anyone within hearing distance. I didn't care. Being able to get this close to the meerkats was magical. They looked like little dogs, so I instantly liked them. Why had it taken me so long to come to the zoo? Right at that moment, a most delicious smell filled my nose. What was that buttery, sweet, yummy smell? I turned around and saw a concession wagon roasting candied almonds.

"Would you like a sample?" the young woman at the cart asked me.

"Sure, thank you," I said, taking one from her little scoop. Only after I put one in my mouth did I wonder how unsanitary it might be. I had to trust my immune system. I crunched up the sweet, crispy nut and swallowed it. "Wow, that's really good. Thanks again."

"Would you like to buy a bag?" she asked.

"No, thanks, not today." The plastic cone of almonds was too much for me to eat and way too expensive, but I was proud of myself for being willing to try one of them. My healthy voice was in charge, and I wanted it to stay that way.

The next exhibit I came to was the flamingos. Before I was close enough to get a good look at them, the smell of a broken sewage pipe nearly knocked me over. As I approached the flamingo exhibit, I realized the smell was coming from them. Was the almond cart strategically planted near the flamingos to cancel out their repulsive smell? As with the meerkat exhibit, there were no bars or windows between the animals and the visitors, which I appreciated. Mostly, the flamingos were just standing there, perched on one leg with the second one pulled up near their round, pink bodies. I moved along.

As I made my way to the next exhibit, I noticed all the lush plant life. Bushes, cacti, flowers, and trees grew abundantly all around. A bench presented itself to me just at that moment, so I sat down to look at the paper map I'd been given at the gate. Once I got my bearings, I knew I wanted to see the polar bears next. Of all the animals on exhibit, I was most interested in seeing the bears and any others that looked like dogs.

The polar bear exhibit had a big moat full of water around it, presumably to keep them from getting out, but the two bears in the exhibit were so comfortably sprawled on the wet pavement, it didn't look as though they had any plans to escape. They looked hot and their fur had a green tinge to it. I would learn later that they turn green because their hair is translucent and hollow, like a straw, and when the weather is warm algae grows inside each hair.

Within minutes of watching the two bears, my childhood fondness for teddy bears welled up inside me, and I knew I'd be back to visit them.

After a couple of hours exploring the zoo, I was tired and ready to go home, but I was also elated to have discovered a new venue for learning. Now I just had to relax for a couple of weeks until my class started.

***

The class met in a big auditorium in the mid-Wilshire area of Los Angeles, which was a pretty gritty neighborhood at night, but I didn't care. I was determined to find a way to work with animals, and I had committed to attending this class every Thursday evening for six weeks. After parking my car on the foreboding gang-banger streets, lined with liquor stores and seedy fast-food joints, I walked defensively from my car to class.

The instructor, an energetic, roly-poly lady, explained all the different types of jobs people had at the zoo, as well as classes and volunteer opportunities available. As I listened to this charismatic dynamo enthusiastically describe the programs, the gears in my head turned round and round, figuring out where I might fit in.

When Miss Roly-Poly explained that paid jobs at the zoo were hard to get, my interest in the volunteer programs grew. Several of them focused on educating the public about the zoo and its non-human inhabitants. That sounded fun, and I wanted to know more. Attending the class for six weeks gave me a good understanding of what it took to run a zoo, and I felt more confident as I explored my dream of somehow working there.

Becoming an animal keeper was not realistic for me, because it required a lot of energy and strength. Applicants for the keeper jobs had to pass strength tests like carrying 50-pound bags of food for 100 yards. Even at my healthiest, I never possessed the brawn required to take care of zoo animals.

The education department interested me a little, but I couldn't picture myself working with children. The department that really got my attention was Research. From what Miss Roly-Poly described, the staff and volunteers studied the behavior of the animals. Although I did not have a lot of confidence in myself physically, I knew I had a good brain and could use it for that.

Before I finished my Introduction to Zoo Operations course, I signed up for the Research class, which would get me started on the road to volunteering. Again my timing was good, because the class was scheduled to start in two weeks. The curriculum included learning techniques of organizing and collecting numerical data of animal behavior and methods of producing accurate descriptions of behavior. After I registered, I eagerly counted the days for the class to start.

Much to my delight, the Research class was held at the zoo. For the next four months, I attended a lecture every Thursday evening. Each week we learned new observation skills and were given exercises that took us to different animal exhibits on zoo grounds to implement our new skills. So in addition to being there Thursday evenings, I went two days a week to do my homework. Because I was not working, I had the luxury of doing my observations either early in the morning or late afternoon, when the zoo was relatively empty and pastoral. Spending a couple of days a week with the animals appeased my anxiety and depression.

"I know you like going to the zoo, but I'm concerned because you look like you've lost some weight. Have you been eating?" Don asked one morning as I was getting ready to go to the zoo.

"Yeah, in fact, I'm more motivated to get calories in, because I want to get through my two-hour shift. If I skip a snack, I get too dizzy," I quickly assured him.

"Okay, just keep working at it," he reminded me. I had told him the truth, but he knew that when I felt good I believed I didn't need much food. Even if I wasn't consciously trying to restrict my calorie intake, my default was to eat as little as possible. But now I was so grateful to have the zoo to look forward to every day that I wasn't going to let myself slip back into depression. That meant I had to eat more.

For our final projects, the class was divided into groups of five. My group was assigned to study the behavior of the female maned wolf during her estrus and gestation periods. The first time I went to observe her, I fell in love. Her name was Lorena and she was beautiful. She had scraggly, red fur and long, black, elegant legs.

The time I spent studying Lorena was spellbinding. I chose to do my two-hour observations at four in the afternoon, because most of the zoo guests were gone then, so I wouldn't be interrupted by their questions. It was only natural for people to be curious about what I was doing there, holding a timer and writing on a clipboard, but they irritated me and broke my concentration.

When I stood at the edge of the exhibit, I was only fifteen feet away from Lorena, so I could see her well. She usually walked into the shady, wooded exhibit, chased crickets and urinated to scent-mark her favorite spots. My job was to record her activities in fifteen-minute increments. We were not permitted to speak to our subjects during our observations, because it would alter their natural behavior, but I imagined conversations I might have with her about her coming mommyhood.

After two months, all five of the groups in class completed their observations and we turned in our data to the Research staff, who compiled it all. Once we had their reports we took the data and created charts and graphs, which we presented to the group in a PowerPoint format. To make the presentations more interesting, we added photos of the animals and music. Even though our findings didn't reveal any remarkable information about the estrus and gestation periods of the maned wolf, we were happy to have completed an official study.

The night of the presentations was special, because I was so proud to be a part of a research team. The professor invited us to contribute refreshments to the reception, and I made sugar cookies in the shape of wolves with orange frosting. Having a desire to bake cookies was a huge surprise for me, since I had not cooked or baked since my anorexic adolescence, but I really wanted to make wolf cookies for our event, because I was so fond of Lorena. But it wasn't the cookies that made the evening unforgettable for me. It was the news we got from one of the keepers shortly before we started the show. Lorena had given birth to three pups. The joy I felt that night for her success and mine filled me with hope. I was hooked on the zoo and resolute to find more ways to get involved.

Next, I jumped into the zoo's volunteer class, a twenty-one-week course that trained volunteers to give tours and educate visitors about the animals in the zoo. Because I was still not strong enough to hold down a job, I devoted most of my time to the class. The zoo was renowned for having one of the most academically rigorous volunteer programs in the country, so I had to hit the books. In the process, I was pleasantly surprised to find that my ability to concentrate and retain information had not been damaged by my anorexia or depression.

During the twenty-one-week course, which met every Saturday from October to April, I found a new home. My love for animals made my commitment to the program easy, but I had to study hard to pass the exams.

One of our assignments was to give tours to groups of school kids. When I first learned about this requirement, I got scared, because I had not been around kids much in my life and didn't know how to talk to them. But I was too invested in the class to let that stop me. I had to trust that things would work out.

When the morning came for me to give my first tour, I gathered my little group of second graders outside the volunteer office and looked at their young faces. They looked at me like I was about to tell them a juicy secret. I remembered how happy I was when I was in second grade, and all a sudden, I felt seven years old again. I knew at that moment that I wasn't going to have any problem giving tours to kids.

As we walked to the first exhibit I jumped right in with my new knowledge, hoping to get an "Eewww" or some giggles.

"Can anyone tell me what the largest living lizard is?"

"The Gila monster?" one little boy guessed.

"Close, but no cigar. The Gila monster is the largest in the United States, but not in the world. Any other guesses?" They all stared at me expectantly. "It's the Komodo dragon. They get to be nearly ten feet long and can weigh about two hundred pounds. That's a big lizard, right? You wouldn't want to keep one of these in an aquarium in your bedroom."

"I have a lizard at home in my bedroom," one little girl proudly told me.

"That's so cool!" I said. When we reached the first exhibit I did a quick head count and asked, "Shall we go inside?"

The kids squealed as we entered the enclosure to see the dragons up close.

"Who do you think is this dragon's worst enemy?" I asked.

"A tiger?" one boy suggested.

"No, not a tiger. A Komodo dragon's worst enemies are his mom and dad! Until they get to be eight months old, the little ones have to learn to climb trees to get away, otherwise their mom and dad will eat them."

The kids looked at the huge, toothy dragons, resting quietly behind the glass, and tried to picture them eating their own children. To lighten things up, I hustled them out of the enclosure into the bright sunlight, and we moved on to the alligator pond.

"Did you know that the American alligator doesn't eat anything from October to May? Could you do that?" I asked.

"No!" they screamed. "Don't they get hungry?"

"Every year their metabolism slows down so much that if they ate, the food in their stomachs would rot and kill them. Weird, right?"

"Yuck!" they groaned. As we moved through the zoo I engaged them with more questions and fun information.

"Is there water in that camel's hump?" one little boy asked as we made our way through the zoo.

"No, it's filled with fat, and their bodies draw from it when they go for a long time without food and water. Be careful, he might spit at you!" I warned them. "A camel will remember you if you treat him badly, or if you just give him a dirty look. Ten years from now he might let you have it with a big gooey glob of spit!

"Speaking of spit, do you know how kangaroos cool off in hot weather? They lick their wrists. Try it sometime. Or you may prefer to cool off like a king vulture. They pee on their legs!"

"Gross!" they screamed.

"Don't try that at home," I warned. At that moment, I looked at my watch and saw that nearly two hours had passed, and I needed to get the kids back to their teachers, who were waiting in a picnic area nearby. Where had the time gone?

"Thank you, Miss Thompson," they said, right before they ran to the picnic tables to devour their lunches.

"You're welcome. Thank you." I waved goodbye and headed back to the volunteer office. I was happy to have given my first tour, but I was even happier to learn how much I loved it. Every Monday morning for the next year. I gave tours to kids and totally enjoyed it.

One Monday, after finishing my tour, I waved goodbye to the kids and headed back to the volunteer office to sign out. But before I got to the office, I started to feel faint. As I looked for a place to sit down, I lost control of my bowels, and suddenly my pants were filled with a warm, smelly substance. Instead of going back to the office to sign out, I slowly walked to my car and prayed I'd make it home safely. Early that morning, I'd had several bouts of diarrhea, so I had thought I was empty.

This was the third time in five days that I had felt faint. I was used to making several fast dashes to the bathroom every morning, but feeling faint was new. I'd never sought help for my intestinal distress, because I was too busy dodging my depression. Volunteering at the zoo had kept my mind off my mental and physical challenges, but when the faint feelings started I realized I needed to find a gastroenterologist. My psychiatrist referred me to the God of Gastroenterology at UCLA, Dr. Weinstein.

When I shared my plans with Don, he graciously offered to drive me to my appointment and I accepted immediately. I knew Don cared about me, but sometimes he was too good at detaching himself from my problems and too respectful of my privacy, and it seemed as though he didn't care. To be fair, I'd never told him how bad my symptoms were, so there was no way he could have known.

The medical offices at UCLA were very busy and crowded, and I was glad Don was with me. As we sat in the waiting room, it started to sink in that two years of diarrhea might be serious. Holding Don's hand gave me hope that I could get better. When the nurse called my name to go in to see the doctor, I was touched when Don wanted to come in with me.

The God of Gastroenterology asked a million questions and looked very concerned. He was accompanied by a group of five medical students, whom he called "fellows." They watched and listened.

"Well, Miss Thompson, we're going to throw the book at you." This translated into me getting a colonoscopy, an endoscopy, stool cultures, and *many* blood tests. He discovered that I had a lot of inflammation throughout my digestive tract and diagnosed me with collagenous colitis. He put me on prednisone for a couple weeks, but when that didn't work he added tincture of opium, a very old-school medication. It made me dizzy and nauseated, but after a month I saw some improvement. My poop was still watery every day, but the episodes were down to two again. I could live with that. I had to, because I wanted to get back to my volunteering job at the zoo.

While I was attempting to regain my strength, a veterinary friend asked me if I knew anyone who would be willing to adopt a three-month old puppy who had been dumped out of a van in a parking lot in North Hollywood. My first response was, "Yes, I do. Me!" It seemed like the perfect thing to help me get better. Don was a little hesitant to take in another dog, but after a little begging, he let me keep the new pup. He knew the positive impact our dogs had had on my health. Like our other dogs, she was a mystery blend of breeds and looked like a sister to Arty, except that her ears flopped down instead of standing straight up. She was about the same size as Arty, fifty pounds, and had the same short, caramel-colored fur. At three months old, her wrinkly face showed that she had some Shar-Pei genes. My vet friend had already named her Dixie, so we kept it. When she first came into the house the other dogs were curious, but there was no aggression from any of them, probably because she was so young.

Dixie was my first puppy. Any other dog I had ever loved and cared for had come to me full-grown. Dixie taught me how much work raising a puppy can be, but she was such a smart, good dog, she made it easy. Taking care of her gave me something to do before I returned to my volunteering at the zoo.

Two months passed as I gave my body a chance to get strong again, and I was eager to get back to the zoo. Jumping right back into touring seemed daunting, so I asked the manager of volunteer programs, Erin, if there was some office work I could do. She had been in my research and volunteer classes, and had started as a volunteer, but after her first year of touring she had been hired to a full-time job in the volunteer office. She and I had had great chemistry from the start, and I always saw her as an older sister. In fact, she was younger than me by nearly a decade, but she was tall and had a commanding presence, so she seemed older.

Erin singlehandedly ran the entire volunteer program, which consisted of nearly 700 volunteers. She worked alone, because the previous manager had recently resigned. Seeing her bend over backwards to hold things together made me want to help. When I offered, she accepted, and for the next two years I helped Erin in the volunteer office two days a week with filing and data entry. Maintaining the files of 700 volunteers was more time-consuming than I'd expected.

One morning, when I got to the office, Erin had a big smile on her face.

"Do you have a minute?" she asked as her smile got even bigger.

"Of course, what's up?" I was curious and found her enthusiasm contagious.

"I have some good news I thought you might be interested in."

"Cool, what is it?"

"I got approval from my boss to hire someone to help me in the office!" she said, clasping her hands together. "Is that something you'd be interested in?"

"You mean a paid position? Heck yes, I'd be interested! Since I've been coming in on a regular basis as a volunteer I feel pretty sure I could work again. Will it be part-time?" I asked, thinking that would be perfect for me.

"Actually, it's a full-time position. Do you think you can handle it?" She looked concerned. I took a quick minute to wrap my head around it, not entirely sure I was ready for full-time work.

"Yes," I blurted out. "I can totally handle a full-time position. I mean, I get to work for you, and you're the best boss in the world."

"Thanks. You already know how to use our database and how everything works. You won't have much to learn. If you could get me a resume in the next couple of days, I'll get it to my boss."

The gears in my head started turning. Did I have an updated resume? If not, I was going to write one as soon as I got home.

Working full time sounded a little daunting, but Erin was right. In the past two years, I had learned a lot of the office procedures, so the real challenge would be making sure I had enough strength to get through the work week. I had not sought full-time work since my hospitalization five years earlier, because my doctors didn't want me jeopardizing my recovery. But when this position came up, it seemed like a healthy fit. I was determined to make it work. I submitted my resume and application the next day, then waited for two weeks as Erin's boss, the president of the company, went through the proper protocol of interviewing candidates.

When I had my interview with the president, I was super excited and surprisingly calm inside. I knew I had to prove to her that I was best candidate. Even though Erin was recommending me, it didn't mean that I would automatically get the job.

Exactly seven days after my interview, Erin called to offer me the job. I'd finally found a viable vocation to replace my acting career. Being able to work in a place where the study and preservation of animals was the paramount focus gave me a sense of purpose as well as comfort and hope.

CHAPTER 6

Doctor's Orders

SETTLING INTO MY NEW job at the zoo came easily and adrenaline kept me going for several years. But regardless of how happy I believed I was, or how well I convinced the rest of the world, my journal entries at the time reflected my truth. The pages were covered with complaints of nausea, relentless diarrhea, depression, and fainting. I didn't disclose the severity of my health problems to anyone at work because I was afraid I'd be fired, but Erin was very compassionate and understanding if I needed time off for personal things, and never gave me any reason to believe that being sick would cost me my job.

Except for prearranged doctors' appointments, I had not taken many sick days from work. Having a job to go to, especially one that I dearly loved, provided structure to my day, which I desperately needed to keep my depression under wraps. Feeling useful was important, and I needed to be around people to keep me from being crippled by my fears. Engaging in conversation with others helped muffle the voices in my head that could destroy me.

My doctor frequently asked me how I was managing at work, and I would proudly proclaim, "Pretty well. It helps keep my mind off being sick." The doctor understood, but reminded me that if I lost more weight, it would be wise to stop working to let my body heal.

Per my doctor's request, I wrote down all my symptoms and all the foods and medications I consumed each day. In the hope of keeping my explosive, draining diarrhea under control, my doctor had me try each of the popular opiates, which were notorious for causing constipation. In an attempt to find something effective that I could tolerate, I tried Percocet, Vicodin, Vicoprofen, Norco, Dilaudid, Oxycontin, tramadol, and Darvocet. However, the tiniest dose of any of them made me woozy. Steroids like prednisone and budesonide were the only drugs that gave me relief from daily fecal explosions, but my doctor worried that being on them for long periods would further weaken my bones and immune system. For my grinding nausea, I tried Megace, ginger, Librax, Levsin, Levbid, famotidine, Zofran, and Donnatal. Sadly, nothing helped.

My internist, a mature but athletic little lady who dressed in a navy blue running suit circa 1979, listened patiently, but didn't seem to know how to rid me of my ailments. From the moment I learned that Dr. Running Suit had a handsome, mid-sized German shepherd who came with her to work every day and hung out in her back office, I liked her. "Little Man," as she affectionately called him, looked just like Gus. During my appointments, we often shared stories about our beloved dogs, and because she remembered that I worked at the zoo, she sometimes even asked me for advice about Little Man's health issues. Her inquiries flattered me, since no doctor had ever asked me for assistance on anything. For Little Man's wellbeing, I happily referred her to a good veterinarian I knew.

Regardless of how much I enjoyed our chats, Dr. Running Suit's lack of experience with anorexic patients left me feeling unmotivated and unmonitored. When I got depressed, I ate less and lost weight, but she never said anything. Maybe she was cleverer than I knew. Maybe she knew that my anorexic mind dictated all my behavior, and I was going to do my own thing and control my intake regardless of what she said. Maybe she knew it was futile to fight my anorexia. I was just disappointed that she didn't have any brilliant ideas on how to help me. Since I had only briefly mentioned my history of anorexia, she may have believed that I was not currently entangled in its web. In her defense, I said very little about my anorexia issues.

My healthy mind craved Dr. Running Suit's attention in the hope that she would provide a cure or some strategy to help me recover. The defiant, anorexic voice in my head really wanted her attention so I could prove that I was succeeding at being a sick person. It said, "Hey, look how skinny I am. Can't you see what a good anorexic I am? Don't I get credit for that?" This part of my brain did not want help, just confirmation of how sick I was. After the effort I had put into emaciating my body and asphyxiating my instincts over the years, one would have thought there was some Anorexia Hall Fame to honor people who achieved dangerously low weights, who lost their teeth, minds, and eventually their lives.

To complicate matters, the healthy part of me wanted to have a happy marriage, rewarding job, and healthy, happy "children" (who, in my case, were dogs). If being a successful anorexic meant being dead, how did I explain my desperate need to be all things to all people?

Anyone with an ounce of sense in their head would have quickly pointed out that my needs were contradictory, which was why I never told anyone what I was truly feeling. One might have asked, "Do you actually want the help you are asking for?" My lack of compliance with medications and deliberate restriction of sufficient nutrition indicated that I didn't want anyone's help. And yet, I was tragically disappointed when my doctor didn't have any brilliant ideas on how to fix me. Having me as a patient must have been a nightmare.

My contradictory thoughts and actions regarding my health would have confounded the best doctors. Since I could never convince anyone why my wacky logic made perfect sense to me, I kept my thoughts to myself.

I had never found another human being who understood or condoned my twisted sensibility, so my only comfort came from my dogs. They didn't question my motives or criticize my flawed logic. They loved me no matter how loony I was, and didn't ask me to change. They depended on me for food and shelter, which meant I needed to be well enough to provide for them, but I was spiraling down physically and emotionally and didn't think anyone could help.

Then something happened that I had been dreading for years. The relaxing walks I took with Gus every day grew short because his hind legs had grown weak and arthritic. Every morning and night he wiggled about, waiting for me to put his leash on, but by the time we got to the end of the driveway, he was exhausted and wanted to go back in. Our little walks were solely for his benefit, not mine. Gus needed my comfort now.

From the moment I had fallen in love with Gus fourteen years earlier at the ASPCA in New York, I had lived in fear of losing him. Having never loved anyone the way I loved Gus, I was certain his death would send me into a depression from which I would never recover. He taught me how to love unconditionally; he taught me that I could love and be loved.

Except for a few times when Gus ingested indigestible items like rocks and fishing hooks, he didn't have many health problems. But in the last few years, he had developed crippling arthritis in his hips. We gave him all the best medicines for pain, but at fifteen years old, his hip joints had badly degenerated.

One night, when Don and I were watching television, Gus started breathing hard. I got up from the couch to sit with him, but as soon as I reached him he struggled to his feet and headed for the door. He wanted to go outside to pee before going to bed, so I opened the door and we went out onto the porch. He did his business and went back inside to lie back down next to the couch. His breathing got more labored, so I grabbed a blanket and settled on the floor next to him.

"I'm going to bed, sweetie," Don said as he turned out the light. "Are you gonna stay with Gus?"

"Yeah, I'm worried about him."

"Me too. Good night."

I curled myself around Gus and we both fell asleep. A couple of times during the night I woke up and felt his belly to make sure he was still breathing. He was warm and seemed to be sleeping peacefully. I moved my hand to his ribcage and felt it moving up and down very slowly. At six o'clock in the morning, he started struggling again to get his breath. I rubbed his right ear, then wrapped my arm around his body to comfort him. He tried to take another breath, then his body went limp. I got my body as close to his as possible, hoping to feel his heart. Underneath his front legs, I felt a faint beat, but then it stopped. I froze, waiting for it to beat again, but he was gone. As his soul left his body, I felt a brief moment of unimaginable peace. I caught a quick glimpse of the celestial existence that Gus was headed for, and I knew he was going to be okay.

My eyes welled up with tears, and I started to cry. As much sadness as I was feeling, I also felt relief. Gus had gone to Heaven. He was no longer in his body. He was no longer suffering. Being with him when he passed was surreal. A minute passed as I lay next to his body. As the sun came up, the room got lighter and the reality of Gus's death started sinking in. I needed to tell Don, so I left Gus on the rug for a minute and went into the bedroom.

"Sweetie . . . " My tears choked off my words.

"What is it, honey?" he asked, waking up more quickly than usual.

"Gus just died." My knees went weak.

"Come here," he said, reaching his arms out to hold me.

My sobbing came on hard. "He died in my arms. I felt his heart stop," I said, remembering how amazing that had felt.

"It's okay. He's in a better place. He had a good, long life." Don was crying now too.

"Can you help me get him in the car?"

"Of course. Should we take him to the vet?"

"Yeah, they can send him to be cremated and we can order a nice urn." Another wave of crying consumed me.

"I'll get a blanket and wrap him up." Arty and Peepers were now at the bedside, sniffing our faces, trying to figure out what our crying was all about. Both of them looked sad too. I think they knew that Gus's dying was painful for us, because they both moped around the rest of the day. Sometimes it looked like they were searching for him, but mostly they looked sad.

Losing Gus shook me up enough to realize that I needed to be more honest with Dr. Running Suit about my struggles so she could help me. When I confessed to her that I wasn't eating much and feeling faint, she worried that my heart may have been damaged from malnutrition and referred me to a cardiologist.

With a little hope in my potentially damaged heart, I made an appointment. As I sat in the heart doctor's waiting room I noticed that I was the only patient in the room under eighty years old. No joke. My illnesses had prematurely transformed me into a senior citizen. At forty-three years old, I was spending as much time in doctors' offices as a sickly octogenarian. How pathetic I was to have surrendered to that. My colitis and malnutrition had worn me down to the point where I was ready to meet my maker. What was even worse was that I was looking forward to it. How did I get to this point?

"Miss Thompson," a nurse with mahogany-colored hair called to me.

I followed her into the examining room and the first thing she did was weigh me, my least favorite activity.

"Seventy-eight pounds." She might as well have said two hundred pounds. Being weighed always freaked me out because I was chronically uncomfortable in my own skin. But it was not about my size; it was about lack of self-love. So I was better off when I didn't look at the scale. How could I weigh seventy-eight when I'd barely been eating?

After I sat in the exam room for ten minutes, a jovial man with the countenance and girth of Luciano Pavarotti entered and extended his big chubby hand toward me.

"Hello Miss Martha!" he exclaimed, exuding warmth and a hearty welcome. His beaming face and clear eyes won my heart straight away. Neither his name nor his dialect told me his country of origin. I was always curious about a person's heritage, because I secretly believed that many cultures other than my own held the secrets to a happy life. The values and mores of our American culture were shallow and, in my opinion, shamelessly fed egomania and self-involvement. When I met someone who was not raised in the United States, I always wanted to know where they were raised. My ability to guess where a person was from was pretty good, but this big cuddly man, whom I affectionately named Dr. Teddy Bear, stumped me. Mostly I was impressed by his apparent zest for life, and I hoped it was contagious. Could some have rubbed off on me from our handshake?

He listened attentively as I tearfully described my recent fainting problem, then he carefully explained the functions of the heart and how he was going to conduct some tests to determine exactly what was going on with my cardiovascular system.

"You are just a kid and your ticker is probably fine, but we'll look inside to find out what is making you have these spells. You have many good years ahead of you, and I will help you enjoy them. Okay, Miss Martha?"

"Okay," I sighed, relieved and excited at the same time. By taking my concerns seriously, he put my mind at ease. His sincerity and gentle style caused me to tear up again, but they were happy tears. He wrote out two orders for some tests, handed them to me, looked me in the eye, and stretched out his big inviting arms to hug me. As surprised as I was that a doctor was hugging me, I eagerly hugged him back. Did he hug all his patients, or just those who looked like they really needed it?

The anorexic in me was surprised and disappointed that he didn't find me pathetic. I wanted to be healed, but at the same time wanted to be left alone to die. I wanted people to care for me, but didn't want to be treated like a baby. I wanted everyone to be open with me, but wanted to keep secrets from them. I wanted them to be concerned, but in an alarmed, dramatic, hopeless way, not in an open-armed, optimistic way. Had I given up on ever being well and healthy again or did I genuinely want to die?

Was Dr. Teddy Bear's optimism really just a way to minimize my situation so he could dismiss me? Did he think I was a hypochondriac? Did he think I was overreacting? My healthy mind jumped back in to refute these paranoid thoughts.

Dr. Teddy Bear's twinkly eyes; full, smiling lips; and large physique were reassuring. Here was a person who embraced life, who loved to eat, drink, and be merry, and who happened to be a keen cardiologist.

In the following weeks, I completed the tests including the echocardiogram, electrocardiogram (ECG), cardiac stress test, Holter monitor, and event recorder. While examining the results, Dr. Teddy Bear shared with me that I had a very slow heart rate, low blood pressure, low blood volume and a thickened valve. None of these things were particularly serious and I was disappointed. The doctor was pleased and hopeful. My anorexia had not yet damaged my heart, which surprised me. Since I had not confided in him about my psychiatric history, he probably thought he was talking to a rational, healthy-minded person who would respond with hope to his news. Forcing a smile, I pretended that I was happy about it. After all, I liked and respected him and wanted him to like me.

At this point, I was ashamed of my anorexia and felt bad for wasting his time. As usual, when I met a new doctor, I prayed that he would present me with some magic cure that would rid my mind of the cruel, self-loathing voices and make me normal again.

Thinking we were finished with our follow-up appointment, I gathered myself together to leave, but he continued to speak and I realized that he was not finished with me. Maybe he had read my medical notes that revealed my history of an eating disorder. Maybe he knew that I was vulnerable and that I needed encouragement.

"Miss Martha, in order to remedy your heart issues, we could install a pacemaker, which would regulate blood flow and hopefully stop the fainting, but since you already have a catheter in your chest for your IVIG, I am reluctant to place any more foreign matter into your frail body. There is too little room on your chest for another device."

"What am I supposed to do about the fainting? Stick close to home? I can't do that, because I need to work. My emotional stability depends on working. I'll go nuts if I have to stay at home!"

"You need someone to watch out for you," he suggested.

"What do you mean? Like a nurse? That would be weird."

"What about another sort of companion?" he asked.

"Huh? I'm not sure I follow." Then my mind flashed on another meaning for *companion*. I looked him straight in the eye and my puppy-loving heart leapt out of my chest. "You mean a dog?" I asked incredulously.

"Yes, a service dog," Dr. Teddy Bear replied in a cursory way. "Do you like dogs?"

"Yeah, I love dogs," I said.

"Dogs can be trained to lick your face, providing 'tactile stimulation' when you feel faint, which can keep you from passing out. They can even help you regain consciousness by doing the same thing. And of course, they can be trained to get help if you need it."

"Really?" I sounded like a little kid, amazed at what I was hearing.

"Just an idea," he said very casually.

"So how would I get one?"

"That is your assignment, Miss Martha. Do your homework and let me know what you find. I am happy to write a letter stating that you would benefit from a service dog."

"Okay, thanks. I will." I was excited when I left his office, but by the time I got home reality hit me. *What are you thinking? You don't deserve to have a service dog. It's a ridiculous idea. Forget it.*

CHAPTER 7

That Yarn Store

EVEN IF I DIDN'T think I deserved a service dog, I needed to make some changes in my life that would help me get healthier. One of my biggest problems was that I had become a workaholic. On my days off I worked from home, and on holidays, when my boss was not there, I snuck into the office to get caught up on things. I had lost the ability to rest and relax. I had lost the ability to have fun. *What makes you think you even deserve to have fun?* the evil voice in my head asked. *If you can't do your job well, you're useless. You are your job. Without it, you're nothing, so don't mess it up.*

The one thing I could still enjoy was walking the dogs with Don. Since we lost Gus, I started helping him walk Arty, Peepers, and Dixie. They needed to walk twice a day, so Don walked them in the morning and I helped at night.

One night as Don and I were heading for bed, Peepers got up from the floor and walked toward the door. Before I could get it open, she fell and started shaking.

"I think she's having a seizure," I said as I put my body on top of hers to keep her from hitting her head. After thirty very long seconds, the shaking stopped. "Peeps, are you okay?" I asked, hoping it was over. Nine years earlier, right after we adopted her, she had had a seizure, but none since then.

"You okay, Peeps?" Don put his hand on her face.

"Her eyes are open, but she's not getting up." At that moment, she tried to get up, but her back legs were not working.

"Should we take her to the emergency hospital?" Don asked.

"Yeah, something's wrong." We wrapped her in a blanket, and Don carried her to the car. The emergency vet was only a mile away, so we got there fast. Thankfully, it was not crowded at midnight. Sitting in the waiting room, I couldn't help but think about the day we lost Gus. It was too soon for Peepers. She was only ten years old.

The vet called us in to the exam room.

"I'm sorry to say that her back legs are completely paralyzed," The vet explained. "She may live, but her quality of life will be poor."

"What should we do?" I asked.

"Euthanizing her is the most humane thing to do."

"Poor Peeps." Don rubbed her neck. "I think it's best, honey."

"I know." I started crying and Don put his arm around me. "At least she'll be with Gus, right?"

"Yeah," Don nodded.

"Okay. I don't want to be in the room," I said.

"I understand. It's okay. I'll stay."

"Goodbye, Peeps." My heart was so heavy, but I didn't want Peepers to suffer.

I put my face on hers and kissed her, then went straight to the car and cried until Don came out ten minutes later.

"She's gone," he said. "She's with Gus now."

"I keep trying to tell myself that I got through the horrible pain of losing Gus and I will get through this too."

"You will. We both will. We've still got Arty and Dixie, and they need us now more than ever." By the time we got home, it was 2:00 a.m. Arty and Dixie greeted us at the door. I hugged each of them, then fell into bed.

Losing Peepers hurt like hell, and I needed to find things to distract me from my pain. Pouring myself into my job more was not a good solution since I already spent too much time obsessing about it, so I started keeping my eyes open for new ways to spend my time. One afternoon as I was driving down a main boulevard near home my eyes fell on a charming, handmade sign above a little store that read, "THAT YARN STORE." The big block letters were painted in primary colors, and looked like they'd been cut out of cardboard by the hands of a child. The playfulness of it drew me in. When had that shop opened? My grandmother had taught me to knit when I was four years old and since then I had found great comfort anytime I picked up knitting needles. However, it had been several years since I had taken the time to start anything. The cheerful yarn store sign and fond memories of knitting with my grandmother moved me to park my car and go inside.

A portly man with a long gray ponytail, scraggly beard, and warm smile said, "He-llo-o!" His voice went from high to low to high again, making *hello* a three-syllable word, and I smiled. The store couldn't have been more than six months old, but it felt lived-in and homey. Even the layer of dust on everything added charm. The wooden shelves against the walls were haphazardly filled with all sorts of wool, including big, bright yellow skeins, perfect for grade school art projects; fuzzy rose-colored mohair balls, which looked expensive; and chunky dark purple skeins for cozy, warm sweaters.

The middle of That Yarn Store was occupied by two worn-out couches, facing each other. Sitting on them were three women and a man, all knitting. Their heads were bowed, and their eyes were focused on their work. A heavyset woman with short, wild, burnt red hair sat in a big recliner. Even though none of them made eye contact, they were engaged in a passionate discussion about the possibility of Barack Obama running for president. Their liberal opinions got my attention and drew me in. A happy thought entered my head: this would be a cool place to hang out. I could have *fun* here.

Half-eaten bags of gluten-free chips, a plate of homemade chocolate chip cookies, and water bottles were scattered on the coffee table between the couches. Had I walked into someone's home? The treats on the table were being enjoyed in a communal manner. Everyone was sharing, which was neat.

"I'm Steven, and who are you?" asked the portly, ponytailed man, the owner of the shop. "Have a seat." His eyes twinkled and he exuded wisdom. Another happy thought came to me: Steven could be my knitting guru.

"Hi, I'm Martha. I love your store! How long have you been here? How come I haven't been in here before today?" My words tumbled out excitedly.

"I don't know," he responded, mimicking my goofy energy. "You're here now. We opened up about a year ago." I wanted to kick myself for not finding this treasure trove before today, but instead I sat down to listen and watch the other knitters. Among them was Paloma, a stout, friendly-faced woman with black curly hair and an olive complexion. Her clever conversation reflected her years as a professor of Latin studies.

Francine, a stay-at-home mom of a ten-year-old boy, was also quite bright and had an interesting history as a lobbyist in Washington.

"Please join us," Francine urged, offering me a pair of needles and some yarn. Her kindness was genuine.

The third woman, Meegan, was close to my age and looked like she could've been my sister. She had shoulder-length, strawberry blond hair and a childlike speaking voice that I found endearing. Meegan was the mother of two teenagers, something I could not relate to, but I soon learned that we shared an intense love of dogs. Ten years earlier she taught elementary school, but left to be a stay-at-home mom. Her children were nearly adults now, but she still spoke like she was addressing small children. Her baby-talk made sense when I learned that she spent all her time fostering homeless puppies for a nonprofit dog rescue.

Francine and Meegan were moms, so naturally their daily experiences were different from mine, but I was delighted to find that we had a lot in common. For one thing, we all lived in Eagle Rock, a section of Los Angeles that was maintaining its small-town feel despite a recent influx of hipsters.

Eagle Rock's provincial atmosphere was surviving because of all the "mom and pop" shops. Half a block from That Yarn Store was an old-timey coffee shop, circa 1967, named Armon's. There, you could get your bacon and eggs breakfast plate for $3.99. And a few doors down from that was a funky, New-Age coffee shop called Swork, where you could sit at a little table with your laptop, write your screenplay and have a soy latte and vegan muffin. A little farther down the street was a Starbucks, if you needed one.

The cultural diversity and tolerance in Eagle Rock were delightfully modern. Predominantly Caucasian and Hispanic, this neighborhood also had a significant Filipino population, so my appreciation for their culture grew. African-Americans and Armenians contributed to the scene as well. Everyone lived together in relative peace, which made me happy.

As we sat on the threadbare couches talking, I learned that these middle-aged ladies and men had curious minds and open hearts, and, dare I say, were oddballs in their own special ways, like me.

***

Twice a week I hung out at That Yarn Store with my new friends. It was a great place to relax on my days off, or after a hard day at the zoo. We sat for hours, knitting and talking. Our conversations covered topics like grumpy husbands, sick dogs, rebellious teenagers, new movies, and current events. When the conversation got too political, I tuned out because I preferred to stay passive and ignorant, but when Meegan gave her reports about the latest litter of puppies she was fostering, I lit up and probed her with questions. I wanted to meet them.

My first visit to Meegan's was on a Saturday, when all the knitters from That Yarn Store came together to hold a yard sale in order to raise money to keep the store open. Selling yarn and imparting knitting wisdom did not pay the bills for Steven, and the store was in jeopardy. This news terrified me because I didn't want to lose my new nest of friends. Those of us who regularly gathered to knit scoured our homes for unwanted, no-longer-needed items we could sell to procure funds to keep the yarn store afloat.

The front yard of Meegan's two-story, lived-in home was covered with items all the knitters had donated to the cause. My old typewriter and unworn t-shirts were among them. Many books, old chairs, and a huge collection of troll dolls and stuffed animals were waiting to be purchased. As I approached the house, my eyes went straight to a puppy pen in the yard, where three fuzzy little black and tan pups were frolicking.

"How old are they?" I asked Meegan.

"Two months today. You want to hold one?"

"Awww, they're so cute. What breed are they?"

"These are Lola's kids, part chihuahua, part dachshund, and a little bit Yorkie," she said with tender enthusiasm. Not being a fan of small dogs, I was a little disappointed and surprised to learn their mix. At two months old, many breeds look alike. They don't develop the distinctive characteristics of their parents for months. Lola had come to Meegan very pregnant, three months earlier, from the rescue organization she volunteered for. The puppies were born into her care, where they would stay until they were four months old. At that time, they would be ready for adoption.

The puppies' floppy ears said, "Aren't we cute?" and their little whimpers said, "Pick me! Pick me!" Two of them were wild and rambunctious, rolling around and squeaking, but one sat quietly, with a quizzical look on his face. He looked me right in the eye, which seemed odd for a puppy, and I was sure he was about to say something to me, like "Hi, how is your day going?"

"Who is this little guy?" I asked, referring to the calm one.

"I think that's Albert," Meegan said, as she turned him over to verify his sex. "Yep, that's Albert Camus."

"Ah, yes, the writer, that's funny. Hi, Albert." I reached down to pet his little round head. He was very docile, but his eyes were bright.

"Here, hold this little girl," Meegan suggested as she handed me Carmen Miranda, Albert's sister.

"No, that's okay. I want to talk to Albert." Our eyes locked. The sincerity of his gaze convinced me right then and there that I could love a little dog. The expression on Albert's face said, "We little dogs have the same capacity to love that big dogs have, you know?"

But there was more to the look in his eyes. His focus stayed on me for an unusually long time and he seemed to be saying "I'd be good for you." Of course, I believed him.

"If Albert goes missing, you better check my house," I playfully warned Meegan when I started fantasizing about scooping him up and taking him home with me.

"They're not ready for adoption yet, but I will keep that in mind," Meegan noted.

"He is so cute!" I said, wanting to cuddle him. He only weighed about two pounds and had black and tan markings similar to those of a German shepherd. His head was way too big for his body, as was the case with most puppies, and he had blond eyebrows above his big, soulful eyes. His floppy little ears, which would eventually stand up straight, enhanced his charm. As I helped with the yard sale for the rest of the afternoon, all I could think about was adopting Albert.

"I'm serious about adopting him," I said to Meegan, hoping she got my drift.

"They need to stay with Lola until they reach four months, but Albert isn't going anywhere. He'll be here waiting for you."

My heart made up my mind for me and I assured her that I was going to adopt him. "Meegan, do you mind if I change his name?" I asked. "Albert is too hard to say."

"Of course I don't mind," she told me. "My daughter and I came up with all the puppies' names when they were born so we could tell them apart, but you can call him anything you want."

"In keeping with the writer theme, I think I'll call him Henry, after Henry Miller. What do you think?" I asked her.

"I like it. From now on, we'll call him Henry."

"All I need to do is talk to Don about adopting him, but I'm pretty sure he'll agree to it."

"Sounds perfect," Meegan said.

"Okay, Henry, I'm going to help with the yard sale, but I'll come back to see you before I leave. God, he's so freakin' cute!"

We raised $400 for That Yarn Store from our sale, which helped Steven pay a few bills, but the next few months were very difficult and it wasn't long before he had to close. For me, though, the yard sale was a blessed event because that was the day Henry came into my life.

CHAPTER 8

Henry Comes Home

WHEN I MET HENRY at That Yarn Store yard sale, I wanted to take him home that day, but I understood the importance of him staying with his mom until he reached four months. Besides, I needed time to convince Don that we needed another dog.

Having a puppy to take care of was going to help me, especially since I was feeling so crappy. My diarrhea was draining the life out of me, and I often felt faint and depressed. Hanging out with my knitting friends gave me temporary relief, as did time with Don and the dogs, but I needed something more. The weaker I got, the less I cared about living, and even though I didn't have a plan to commit suicide, I was gradually starving to death. But after meeting Henry, and getting the idea to adopt him, my hope of getting better returned. I went back to see Dr. Teddy Bear for help.

"Miss Martha, your weight is dangerously low. Your heart is in jeopardy." Dr. Teddy Bear warned.

"I know, but when I eat, my diarrhea gets worse. Eating just makes me more miserable." I tried to explain.

"Have you heard of TPN, Miss Martha?" Dr. Teddy Bear asked.

"I don't think so, why, what is it?" I was relieved that he had a possible solution.

"Total parenteral nutrition. It's a way for you to get nutrition without involving your gastrointestinal tract. It goes directly into your blood through your port. You have a Port-A-Cath, right?" he asked, referring to the port I had in my chest for my monthly IV immunoglobulin treatments.

"Yeah, right here," I said, pulling the neck of my shirt down to reveal the knob on my chest that looked like a peculiar, small, misplaced third breast.

"Would you be willing to try something like that?"

"I'd give it a try, sure." As complicated as it sounded, I was game because I wanted to have more energy.

"You will feel much better," he said confidently. Then he paused, looked me in the eye and said, "You've got many good years ahead of you, Miss Martha."

His warm smile and steadfast optimism made me believe I might get better.

"I will place the order and arrange for you to meet with the nurse who will teach you how to administer the TPN."

"Thank you, Doctor," I said as he walked me to the reception desk. Would he give me a hug like last time? I hoped so because I wanted to show him my appreciation. He was saving me. As much as I wanted to hug him, I resisted because I was afraid his staff would think I was weird. Did any of his other patients find him huggable? He placed his big paw on my shoulder and wished me well. That would have to do.

The next day, a nurse came to our house with all the supplies and taught me how to hook up my TPN. With great care and patience, she showed me how to sterilize all the tubes and syringes I would use to flush my port. She emphasized that I needed to be extremely careful, because any germs or bacteria that entered through my body could kill me, since my port led straight to my heart.

In order to infuse the TPN, my port had to be accessed 24 hours a day, 7 days a week. The nurse went through her supplies and pulled out the special needle that would be inserted into my catheter. It looked like a big pushpin. The base was a plastic disc, an inch in diameter, and it had a thick needle sticking out that was an inch long. The entire needle would be inserted into the port that lived underneath the skin above my right breast.

"This may hurt a little." Standing directly in front of me, the nurse positioned her legs evenly to get good leverage, then she held the needle on top of the port. "Okay, one, two, three . . . " As swiftly as she could and with a great deal of pressure, she pushed it perpendicularly into my port.

"Ahhhhh!" I tried to muffle my scream as the needle entered my chest. Once the needle was far enough in, the pain stopped, but I stayed tense.

"It's in," she assured me, then covered the needle with three sterile gauze pads and placed a clear plastic shield over the whole port. Now I had a tent on my chest that stood two inches high.

"Are you okay?" she asked. I still had my eyes tightly closed and was holding my breath.

"Yeah, I'm fine," I exhaled. "How often do I get to go through this?"

"We'll change it once a week." Next, she showed me how to attach the nozzle of the TPN bag to the little tube that came out of my port. Again she emphasized that I needed to rub the nozzles with an alcohol pad for at least fifteen seconds. She counted to fifteen each time she showed me, and I got the point.

TPN was a milky, viscous liquid, prepared by the pharmacist and put into 1000 ml clear plastic bags that resembled hot water bottles. It smelled like baby formula. Seven bags would be delivered once a week in a cooler to our house, and I would have to put them immediately into the refrigerator. The nurse explained that my TPN formula was prepared specifically for my nutritional needs and was chock full of proteins, dextrose, electrolytes, and minerals. Every night before bed, I would hook up one of the bags of TPN to an infusion pump, which I would put into a backpack that would sit on a little chair next to the bed.

The pump that made the TPN flow through the tube was the size of the Sony Walkman I had had in the '80s, but significantly heavier. The nurse taught me how to program it to infuse 1000 ml over a twelve-hour period. At the end of the twelve hours I would go through all the steps of sterilizing and flushing my port again.

As complicated and risky as TPN sounded, I was hopeful that it would help. My body would finally get proper nutrition, but I wouldn't have to experience the nausea, cramping, or splattery diarrhea that came with eating. Taking this step to help myself made me feel proud and lifted me out of self-pity. I had to get my strength back, because Henry, our new puppy, would soon need me.

***

When Henry reached four months, Meegan recommended that I take him home for a "play date" to meet Arty, Dixie, and Don. Convincing Don that we needed another dog was not hard. Perhaps he recognized that my will to live was fragile and that a puppy could be my ticket back to health. Perhaps he remembered the positive impact that Dixie had on me after my fainting started. Adopting Dixie when she was just three months old had restored my will to live, so welcoming little Henry into my life now would hopefully have the same affect.

On the day of Henry's scheduled play date, I sped through my morning prep because I was so eager to get him. Life was beautiful. As soon as I got to Meegan's house, she placed Henry in my arms. I kissed his little black head and sat him in the passenger seat of my car. At four months old, Henry was four pounds of solid cuteness. Although I was not terribly concerned, the "play date" was important so we could make sure that Arty and Dixie would accept Henry. After I made sure he was settled next to me, we went home.

We entered through the front door, and I put Henry down on the wooden floor of the living room. He leaned into my legs for protection. Dixie and Arty came bounding over to sniff him out, but they were cautious and gentle. His teeny body looked especially small next to the two fifty-pounders as they carefully explored his puppy odors. Henry looked up at me, and I assured him that he'd be fine by placing my hand on his little round forehead. After ten seconds of cautious sniffing of Henry's hindquarters, both Dixie and Arty wagged their tails and lowered their chests to the ground, indicating that they wanted to play. In silence, Henry rotated his ears back and briefly raised his hackles, but when he saw that the other dogs only wanted to play, he sat down behind me and leaned on my leg.

Don stepped into the living room from the kitchen, where he was grinding the rich, aromatic beans for his extra-bold coffee. Henry was content at my feet. My timing was perfect, because Don's mood was always good while he was preparing his morning brew. Coffee time amplified Don's already buoyant nature, which I deeply appreciated and believed was one of the reasons I had not dissolved into total self-destruction in recent years. This morning he appeared to be his usual cheerful self, and I was hopeful that he would like Henry.

"He's so docile," Don said with a smile. *That's a good sign,* I thought.

"Yeah, he really is. Isn't he cute? And look, Dixie and Arty have accepted him."

"Aw. Hey, little guy, come here." Don reached down to pick him up. We had never had a small dog. Seeing Don tenderly hold Henry was touching because he was so gentle. He loved me with the same gentleness. The smile on Don's face told me that Henry had found a home in his heart, and I was confident that my decision to adopt him was a good one.

Henry's play date was a success, and when I took him back to Meegan's, I told her the good news.

"All we need to do is complete the adoption papers and you can take him for good," Meegan explained.

"How long will that take?" I asked, hoping she would say "Five minutes."

"If you want to come back tomorrow morning we can seal the deal," she said.

"Fantastic! I can't wait to take him home. Don, Dixie, and Arty loved him. I promise he'll have a good home." I went straight home to give Don the good news.

As planned, I brought Henry home the next day. When he explored the house, Dixie and Arty watched him, but didn't try to intimidate him or prevent him from settling in. When either of them approached to give him a sniff, he stopped what he was doing to look at them, but didn't growl or run away. At four pounds, he looked so tiny and vulnerable next to them. As I moved around the house, he followed me, and I was terrified that I would forget he was there and step on him. Unlike Arty and Dixie, whose presence I could feel and hear, Henry was silent and barely cast a shadow. I worried I might squish him if I backed up suddenly or changed direction. So I made a conscious effort to keep him in view.

We got out the big Vari-Kennel crate that Gus used to travel in, and set it up in the kitchen for Henry to learn potty training. But after the first day, it wasn't necessary, because Henry was sharp as a tack and quick as a whip. He was housebroken within forty-eight hours of coming home. Of the five dogs I had ever owned, Henry was definitely the smartest.

"Have you noticed how smart he is?" I asked.

"Yeah, he's pretty quick for a little guy," Don agreed.

"Do you remember when I told you that Dr. Teddy Bear had recommended that I get a service dog?" I asked excitedly, as an idea sprouted in my mind.

"Sure, a couple of months ago, right?"

"Do you think Henry could be a service dog? I mean, do you think little dogs can be service dogs?"

"I don't know, but I'm sure you could find out," he said as he touched my cheek with his hand.

"I know what I'm doing today." I sat up, grabbed my TPN backpack and went to feed the dogs. I was on a mission.

CHAPTER 9

Service Dogs 101

WITHOUT WASTING ANY TIME, I started researching the world of service dogs. Was Henry big enough? If so, who could train him? Did I need to be trained too? How much would it cost? What kind of documentation would we need? Would Henry need to wear a special vest? I had so many questions, but when I imagined Henry helping me, my energy and optimism surged.

The best source of information I found was the Americans With Disabilities Act (ADA) website.[1] It provided answers to common questions, addressing the definition of service animals and general rules for use; requiring no national certification or registration; describing policies for employers and business owners and the rights and responsibilities of service dog owners.

My eyes scanned through the 35 questions and I found exactly what I wanted:

Question #22. Can service animals be any breed of dog?

Answer: Yes. The ADA does not restrict the type of dog breeds that can be service animals.

This was great news because Henry was a "dachs-huahua" or "chi-weenie," a mix of two small breeds. So even when he was full grown, he would be significantly smaller than any service dog I'd ever seen.

Next, I looked for answers about training. I was relieved to find this:

Question #5. Does the ADA require service animals to be professionally trained?

Answer: No. People with disabilities have the right to train the dog themselves and are not required to use a professional service dog training program.

Since I had no idea how to train Henry, I wanted to find a professional who knew what they were doing. The ADA website provided a lot of great information, but didn't give any recommendations or referrals for *where* to could get training. Were there any schools nearby? Was he even trainable? Was he smart enough? If I found a teacher, would I be strong enough to go through the classes with him?

Fortunately, my curiosity overrode my ignorance and naïveté. My appreciation for the healing power of animals had started with Gus, and I knew that any effort I made to get Henry trained would be worth it.

After clicking and scrolling on the Internet for a couple of hours I learned that I had two choices. I could send Henry to a special school to be trained, which could cost as much as $20,000, or I could hire a private teacher who could train us as a team for less than $3,000. I narrowed my search and found a local trainer with a strong background in animal behavior and performance training. Her name was Penny Scott-Fox, and she owned and operated Scott-Fox Dog Training. According to her website, she was one of the nation's most respected dog behavior specialists. She was also one of the founding instructors for Certified Nose Work Instructors (CNWI). She helped popularize the sport of K9 Nose Work in Southern California, and taught nosework teams for all levels of competition. I was impressed to see that she'd been the Behavioral Director for the Pasadena Humane Society in Pasadena for twelve years, and was a fellow of the Pet Behavior Institute in Durham, England.

When I called Penny's office she invited me to stop by that afternoon at 4. So I put Henry in his little crate and drove to her school, which was situated in the foothills of Altadena, just north of Eagle Rock. Her ratings on Yelp were all four and five stars and her business seemed well-established. The reception area was very cheerful and welcoming. Behind it were several large training rooms, all which were very clean. Above the reception desk was a board listing the complex schedule of all the classes she taught, including three levels of obedience: service and therapy dog training, nosework, and agility training. The same board listed the names of her staff members, who were also experienced trainers. From what I could see, she knew what she was doing.

In addition to her impressive credentials, Penny was very personable. As I listened to her talk about her training philosophy I could see she was bright and had a good sense of humor. When she spoke about all the classes she offered and explained her teaching philosophy, I was startled at how direct and strict she was, but I figured she had to be in order to be so good at it. She had a no-nonsense approach to her work, which I respected, but she also had a twinkle in her eye and a welcoming smile. I liked her. She was firm but friendly.

When I told her why I needed a service dog and described my physical and emotional difficulties, she listened and nodded with understanding. She didn't pass judgment or ask any meddling questions about my condition. Henry and I were in good hands, and I was confident that our money would be well spent.

***

I didn't sign Henry up for training right away because I wanted to ask Erin if it would be okay for him to come to work with me. The ADA website stated that zoos could legally refuse access to service dogs in specific areas. This made total sense, because I knew that animals living in the exhibits could get agitated by a visiting dog. A hungry lion might get ideas about jumping his moat, or a young Speke's gazelle might panic, bolt to the fence, and break one of its delicate legs. The coward in me didn't want to ask Erin about the zoo's policy on service animals for fear of being turned down, but I knew how much she loved dogs, and I was excited to tell her about Henry's teacher.

"Do you have a minute?" I nervously asked as I stepped into her office.

"Yeah, sure," she said with a look of concern. Erin was a very compassionate boss and always had time for me. In the past, when I had asked for a few minutes of her time behind closed doors, it had been to request time off for medical appointments and hospitalizations, so her concerned expression was warranted.

"It's nothing bad; I'm fine," I assured her.

"Okay . . . " she said with growing curiosity.

"I told you that I recently adopted a puppy, right?" I reminded her.

"Yes, Henry. How is he?" she asked, smiling.

"He's good, thanks. So, you know I've been having problems with fainting, right?"

"Yes . . . " Her smile was replaced by another look of concern.

"Well, a few months ago, my doctor recommended that I get a service dog to assist me when I felt faint."

Erin's eyes widened.

"And I've been thinking about getting Henry trained to help me. Do you know the zoo's policy on service dogs for employees?"

"I don't know, but I'll find out for you. I have a meeting with Kai this afternoon, and I'll bring it up," she said with genuine enthusiasm. Erin had a big German shepherd whom she adored, so I knew she liked dogs. She also had an open mind and loved the challenge of unconventional ideas. Her optimism had kept me afloat for years. If there was a way to get Henry on board at the zoo, she would find it. She just needed to find out what the rules were. I knew that patrons were allowed to bring in service dogs if they signed an agreement stating they would not go to restricted areas, but Henry would be the first employee service dog.

"Thank you. I'm meeting with his teacher tomorrow. I'll find out more about the whole process and wait to hear from you," I said, feeling encouraged by Erin's spirited reaction.

"This is so exciting," she said with a big smile on her face, bringing her hands together under her chin as if she was about to start clapping. "Hopefully, I will have an answer for you in the next couple of days."

While waiting to hear back from Erin, Henry and I returned to Penny's school. She needed to assess his disposition to make sure he was a good candidate for training. She explained that it was critical that he not show fear or aggression toward humans or other dogs. When I introduced Henry to Penny, she greeted him warmly, scratched him under the chin then led him by the leash into one of the classrooms, where he could not see me. Nervously, I waited five long minutes for her to complete the assessment. She came back smiling, said that he had passed and could take the first class, which was Basic Obedience. Once he completed and passed the six-week course, Penny would do another assessment to determine if he was suitable for further training as a service dog. If he did well, we would have private lessons with her for six months, where he would learn specific tasks to help me.

***

Erin got the green light from the zoo's top brass for Henry to join me at work once he was trained. A personnel file would be created for him, and I would have to provide documentation annually showing proof that he was vaccinated and tested for parasites. The human resources department also asked for a copy of the letter my doctor had written indicating that I would benefit from the help of a service dog.

As soon as we got the okay, Henry and I went to the Parks and Recreation building in the foothills of Altadena, where Penny held her Basic Obedience classes. For some of her training, she preferred to work in a public park so the dogs would be exposed to real world elements like cars, lawnmowers, kids, and other dogs. In our first class, Henry was shy and clung to the back of my legs. There were six other dogs in class, including a rambunctious golden retriever and a couple of poodle puppies. Some people were there just to teach their young dogs good manners and others, like Henry and me, were hoping to earn our Canine Good Citizen certificate. Without this, we couldn't proceed with the service dog training.

During the evening classes, Penny demonstrated how to teach our dogs simple things like *Sit, Stay,* and *Halt.* Using her own dog, a border collie named Harry, she showed us how to give commands using voice and hand signals. When Harry demonstrated the activity correctly, she gave him a little treat. After she showed us, she had each of us try with our own dogs in the presence of the group. From the first class, I could see that Henry was a quick study, and I was happy to discover that he stayed focused and serious for the entire hour.

Once we started classes, Henry and I diligently practiced our lessons for an hour at home every morning, then for another hour when I got home from work. For our evening practice sessions, we went to public places like Petco stores and city parks, where Henry could learn to obey commands with all the distractions of the real world.

The classes and practice sessions took a lot out of me physically, but Henry's brilliant response inspired me to keep going. He would be a huge help once he learned specific tasks to help me, and I was already starting to feel the healing benefits of his presence. Henry's energy ignited my will to live: for the first time in months, I was more willing to eat and wanted to thrive.

Long before we completed his formal training, Henry instinctively knew how to comfort me. One afternoon early in his training, I was feeling faint and got in bed in the middle of the day for a nap. Within ten seconds, Henry came into the bedroom, jumped onto the bed and rushed to me in a serious, investigative manner. He looked me in the eye and started licking my face aggressively. His body language was distinctively different from his play mode. His matter-of-fact posture frightened me, it was so sincere. His little wet tongue tickled my face and neck, and I started laughing, but he kept at it until I said, "Okay, Henry, I'm okay." When he stopped the licking, he backed up, sat down, and stared at me.

"Seriously, Henry, I'm okay. Thanks, guy. What a good boy! Where did you learn to do that?"

Somehow, he recognized that being flat on my back in the middle of the day was not normal. He also knew that when I got in bed at night, I was okay and he'd curl up next to me and go to sleep. For months after that first naptime reaction, he went into high alert every time I got in bed for a nap. When I told him I was "okay," he'd back up, sit down and watch me. I never discouraged his impulse to help me, even though I wasn't in distress. His instinct to monitor me was impressive. Of the four dogs Don and I had owned prior to Henry, some had regularly gotten in bed with us at night, but none of them had been so in tune with me.

When I met with my psychiatrist, Dr. Rose, for my regular monthly visit, I was excited to tell her how well Henry was doing in his training. Before I could get the words out, she took the wind out of my sails. "You look exhausted. Are you okay?"

"I'm fine. In fact, I wanted to tell you how well things were going with Henry's service dog training."

"I'm sorry, I don't mean to burst your bubble, but you look like you've lost more weight. Why don't you take a leave of absence from work while training Henry?" she urged.

"What if I just worked part-time for a while? Would that help?" I asked, knowing that my depression would blaze if I didn't have the daily structure that work provided.

"It might, but promise me you'll take time off if the stress gets to be too much," she bargained.

"Okay," I said halfheartedly. There was no way I was going to completely let go of the safety of my job. Being with my friends at work and helping the volunteers kept me from getting depressed. But working a five-hour day instead of eight would give me more time and energy to train Henry. Dr. Rose was right: I was weak and exhausted, and I had gotten dangerously good at pushing through it.

"I'll write a letter to your employer stating that I am ordering you to reduce your hours to no more than twenty per week. I'll indicate in the letter that I'll re-evaluate your health after two months. Just let me know the fax number," she said.

"Okay, thanks. I'll email it to you."

"But you have to promise me you'll stop working completely if you keep getting weaker. I'll need to see you again in a month."

"Thank you for all your help, Dr. Rose," I said as I left her office. I felt good about this change. Training Henry and working full-time was too much for me, but I didn't want to give either of them up.

Once I switched to part-time, Dr. Rose reminded me that I had to resist the temptation to return to full-time work until I beefed up and got my strength back. *Could I be fired for being sick?* When I presented Dr. Rose's letter to our human resources person, a big hearted, overworked woman named Kai, she saw the fear in my eyes and assured me that my job was safe even if I had to work part-time indefinitely.

"You do not need to worry, my dear," Kai said. "You are a valuable employee, and you will always be welcome here. We want what is best for you."

She's just saying that. You're not a valuable employee. You're wimpy and weak.

Losing so much of my physical strength made me vulnerable, and my fears got more irrational. When I was down, my imagination went to dark places and invented things to be afraid of, such as being fired for having health problems. I had no evidence on which to base this fear, and yet it was alive and well.

As Henry and I went through training, I started getting nervous about what would happen when he came to work with me. Would he be welcome? Would he annoy people? Would his presence generate gossip about me being sick? Erin had known for several years about my frequent doctor appointments, monthly IVIG, and weight loss, but I had deliberately kept quiet about my depression, because I feared I'd be misunderstood and judged. Nobody knew my diagnosis or the specifics, but they could see something was wrong with me. Kai and Erin were always tactful and benevolent in their responses to any disclosure I had made when requesting sick leave, and I had always trusted them. But now fear was creeping into my heart, and I worried my illness might jeopardize my job.

When I expressed my fears about Henry to Kai, who was a great advocate for employee rights and happened to love dogs, she shared her genuine enthusiasm about Henry joining the zoo family. She was sincere and I was relieved, but within moments of leaving her office, the self-loathing, self-doubting entities were back in my head. *If you think you can start bringing a service dog to work, you are out of your mind. It's a ridiculous idea. What makes you think you are so special that you deserve to have a service dog? Get real. Get a grip. You're not sick or disabled; you're just a big baby.*

To quiet my unsound thinking, I put Henry's leash on and took him out to practice our lessons. We were a good team, and he was always willing to review what we'd been learning.

When Henry was only eight months old, we completed the Basic Obedience classes, took the test, and passed the AKC (America Kennel Club) Puppy Test. This was the first step toward his official certification. Good boy!

Henry's "Retail Lessons" were by far the most joyful part of our training because Petco welcomed "dogs on leashes." The nearest branch was just a few miles from home, so it was easy to get to, and it was the perfect place to practice his basic obedience and challenge his concentration. Going to Petco gave him a chance to learn how to navigate a minefield of new dogs, impetuous children, and menacing shopping carts.

After parking in the underground lot below the shopping complex, I strapped on his little blue training vest, filled my pockets with Beggin' Strips, his favorite snacks, and we headed into the store. His teacher was a big proponent of treat training, and Henry was very responsive. Beggin' Strips looked like waxy strips of bacon and possessed the distinctive aroma of fried pork. They were easy to break into tiny bits, so I could keep his attention for a couple of hours without filling him up or making him fat.

When we first visited Petco, Henry's little black body stiffened and he clung to my left calf as we stepped onto the sidewalk in front of the store. The minute I gave him a command and put him in a sit-stay to my left, he straightened up and looked at me. Although he was on high alert for potential threats, like unwieldy children and aggressive dogs, my commands distracted him and he was very obedient, which made me proud. He listened well, but I felt guilty for making him walk through his fears.

We marched up and down the aisles as I repeated the commands: *Halt, Sit, Stay*, and *Heel*. Henry listened intently and I praised him repeatedly with my voice and vittles. In order to become a full-fledged service dog, he needed to have unwavering concentration wherever we went in the event I needed his help. This would be so useful if I had a fainting episode or panic attack in a public place or at work.

Henry's rapid progress in training built his confidence as well as mine. On days when my heart was heavy, our practice sessions helped me carry on. Training was exhausting, but always gratifying.

Henry quickly learned the first four commands, which we

could practice anywhere. In public places we started worked on *No Barking, No Aggressive Behavior,* and *No Intrusion Into Another Person's or Dog's Space.* He was smart, he got it, but we practiced faithfully because we needed to pass the certification test. Training was not easy, and even though I got really excited when I shared information with friends and family about our goals and progress, there were many dreary mornings when I dragged my pooped-out body to the car. Henry's limitless enthusiasm encouraged me to drive to the park so we could work with Penny two mornings a week. With her, we demonstrated what we had been rehearsing every morning and evening. My physical strength faltered frequently, and I was usually lightheaded, but every time Henry performed, I relaxed and felt good about our hard work.

When Henry turned one, we took the test for his Canine Good Citizen certification. Since we'd been practicing so much, he passed on his first try. Now we were ready to start working on the skills he needed to assist me when I fainted or had a panic attack.

The IAADP website provided a list of specific tasks that service dogs needed to learn so they could help their person. Penny and I referred to these for our lessons.[2] One was "Go Get Help," which meant he would know how to summon help from my coworkers and supervisor. Because of my fainting problem, that was a critical skill for Henry. In the event that I felt faint or started to lose consciousness, he knew to bark, lick my face, and go find the nearest person for help.

He also learned to "Provide Tactile Stimulation," "Disrupt Overload," and "Lap Up.: In the event that I felt too weak to manage the demands of people in public or at work I could command Henry to "Lap Up," which would prompt him to put his paws on my legs or jump into my lap, if I was sitting. His presence on my lap would ground me and help me focus on the task at hand. He was taught to remain in place until I calmed down enough to resume normal activity.

"Panic Prevention" was the task Henry learned to keep intimidating people at a distance by placing himself between them and me. After I gave him the command "Down" and used a special hand gesture, he would strategically sit where an aggressive or threatening person could not get close enough to hover over me, consequently preventing panic or a possible fainting episode. My sensitivity to people standing too close was unusually high and I got extremely anxious if someone encroached on my personal space. Even when people approached with benevolent energy, I often felt as though I was going to suffocate.

If someone at work appeared at my desk and angrily complained about something, I would start to panic and feel faint. There was never anything personal about what they were reporting, but I took their complaints very personally. If they didn't like something about our department or the institution, I felt like I had disappointed them and I worried about how I was going to fix it. My thinking would get irrational and I'd have a hard time getting back on track. My hope was that Henry's presence would keep me grounded and prevent me from coming unhinged in these situations.

Henry would be the first employee service dog in the history of the zoo, and our human resources department had to explore the requirements and responsibilities they would need to follow. They also familiarized themselves with my rights. Even though I was excited about Henry helping me, I felt guilty for making them do additional work on my behalf. Kai and the rest of the HR staff were quick to reassure me that they were excited about Henry getting started. The next step for us was to pass the formal test for service dog certification.

CHAPTER 10

The Big Test

OUR BIG DAY CAME. Henry and I were scheduled for the final service dog test. A colleague of Penny's named Jim met us in the park where we had attended lessons. Jim was an experienced service dog evaluator, and an athletic man in his mid-thirties who carried himself with confidence. His casual khaki shorts, sky-blue polo shirt, and well-worn running shoes put me at ease. Prior to meeting him, I envisioned a no-nonsense, stiff-collared evaluator like the guys who gave DMV driving tests. Jim was sincere and focused, but not intimidating. Henry and I were fortunate to find an evaluator close to home. Not all dog trainers possessed the credentials for service dog testing, and it could have been much harder to find someone to evaluate Henry.

After introducing himself to me, Jim read through a checklist of items to make sure Henry and I qualified as a "team" to take the Service Dog Test.

These requirements included:

- I had to show proof that he had passed the Canine Good Citizen Test no earlier than his first birthday.
- Henry had to be wearing his license tag and an identification tag with his name and phone number engraved.

- I had to provide a certificate from his vet proving that he was neutered.
- He had to have completed his training to perform service tasks related to my medical and psychological needs.
- He had to be clean and properly groomed.
- He had to be wearing a flat collar (no prong collars).
- His leash had to be no longer than six feet in length.
- I had to have clean-up supplies (paper towels, plastic bags, pooper scoopers, etc. and a portable bowl and fresh cold water).

Thankfully Penny had gone through this list with me two weeks earlier, so we were prepared. Check, check, and check.

Next, Jim had us demonstrate specific aspects of our training. He asked us to perform at least three service-related tasks to mitigate my disability. We started with Panic Prevention, which was simple and quick. To appear as though I was close to having a panic attack, I started breathing hard and fast, then sat on the ground so I could give Henry the command, "Lap Up." This prompted him to get in my lap and lick my face. Because he responded so quickly, I wrapped my arms around his little body, held him close and said, "Good boy." His warm, furry body in my arms combined with this immediate presence in my face had a profound calming effect and my breathing slowed.

To show Henry's knowledge and ability to respond to a more serious situation using the command "Go Get Help," I dropped to the ground, patted my thighs and started with "Lap Up." Henry responded by jumping to my lap and licking my face. I feigned a faint by closing my eyes, bowing my head and letting my knees buckle so that I dropped to the ground. Then I lay motionless on my back. At this point he licked my face more aggressively, but I didn't stir, so he started barking. He then ran toward Jim and barked some more. Good job, Henry!

Jim watched to make sure that Henry obeyed commands on his first attempt at least 90% of the time. He also paid attention to Henry's ability to maintain a good heel on his leash. Jim asked for me to have Henry lie quietly beside me without creating an obstacle to others. And finally, he confirmed with me that Henry knew to urinate and defecate only in appropriate, designated places. Remarkably, since the beginning of our time together, he'd never had any pee or poop accidents and seemed to know when and where to go. Unlike Arty, who peed anywhere, anytime, Henry had been potty trained almost instantly. He didn't mark his territory with pee and didn't go more than a couple of times a day, which I found odd, compared to Arty's twenty times a day.

"Okay Miss Thompson, here is a list of the important things I look for during the test." He handed me a list:

- The selected service tasks were appropriate for Henry.
- I used only positive reinforcement techniques, verbal and treats.
- I was consistent in enforcing commands.
- I always ensured that Henry was within two feet of me at all times, except when a task required a greater distance.
- I always ensured that Henry had adequate space in order to avoid injury to the dog or others in public.

He then evaluated Henry's public behavior. Because we were in a big public park on a Saturday afternoon, there were numerous opportunities to interact with people.

He verified that Henry would:

- Not solicit attention from strangers.
- Be able to work quietly in public without barking, whining, or otherwise creating a distraction.
- Not growl, snarl, or demonstrate any aggression towards people or other dogs.
- Not solicit or steal food items from the general public.
- Urinate or defecate only in appropriate, designated places.

Henry was not the only one being tested that day. I also had to demonstrate that I could:

- Set and enforce consistent boundaries and prevent members of the public from petting or greeting Henry while he was working.
- Respond politely and appropriately to public inquiries and challenges at all times.
- Maintain control over Henry at all times.
- Remain alert for signs of danger and remove Henry from dangerous situations when necessary.
- Provide Henry with adequate food and hydration, but not feed him in designated public dining areas.
- Provide regularly scheduled rest breaks for Henry.

For an hour, I was in high gear, and I listened and responded anxiously to Jim's instructions. He was kind, friendly, and very efficient. Henry and I stayed on our toes, all thirty of them, to make sure we didn't miss a beat. After Jim went through the list of my responsibilities as a member of our "team," he said we were done and that we could take a break while he made notes and prepared his decision for us.

He walked to a picnic table twenty feet away and sat down with his clipboard and pen. My heart pounded out of my chest. Did we pass? I didn't need to "take a break," I needed our results! Henry's big, brown Chihuahua bug-eyes peered at me and said:

"It's okay, Mommy. Don't panic. We're going to be fine. Come on, let's go sit in the grass and enjoy the park."

Once we settled into a shady spot under a tree, I revisited everything we had been asked to do in the past hour. Henry had been very obedient during the entire test, except for his interest in the other dogs in the park. His gaze got fixed on a couple of dogs playing about fifty feet away and had growled at them twice, but his little growl had been nearly inaudible, thank goodness.

Ten minutes passed while we sat in the grass waiting for Jim's decision. He signed his name to the bottom of the document and stood up. From his clipboard, he removed two sheets of paper, held them in his left hand and walked to us. As fast as I could, I got to my feet. I was breathing hard in anticipation. I almost needed to ask Henry to Lap Up, but I didn't want to interrupt Jim's news.

"Congratulations, Ms. Thompson, you and Henry passed."

"All right! Thank you so much!" I said as I reached my hand to shake his. "We passed, Henry! Good boy!" His little mouth was open, probably because he was panting, but it looked like he was smiling.

"I just need your signature in a few places." Together we walked back to the picnic table to complete the paperwork. I was so proud of Henry. I was so proud of both of us. He was fully trained and tested service dog and we were a proven team.

***

The next day was bright and sunny as I got up to get ready for work. Don was out walking Arty and Dixie, but Henry was there to keep me company. Filled with hope and confidence, I eagerly ate my Cream of Wheat. My enthusiasm to live these days was fueled by Henry's presence and our recent success getting trained. Consequently, I was more willing to follow my doctor's orders and comply with my TPN feedings.

On bad days, when I felt discouraged or when my anorexia was calling, I skipped my TPN. But for the past couple of days, I'd had the sense to recognize that infusing my prescribed 1200 calories of TPN was my only hope of ever getting past my unexplained daily fainting spells.

Being on TPN was a big hassle, because I had to prepare the pump and hook up twice a day, then carry around the special backpack designed to hold the pump and bag of liquid nutrition. Maintaining the port on my chest required time and careful attention because the needle accessed my subclavian vein, putting me at high risk for scary infections like sepsis. My novice nursing skills were pretty good, but sometimes I got cavalier and skipped the whole process of preparing and infusing. My anorexia told me I could survive without consuming any calories. How could I argue with the fact that I was still alive after decades of consuming fewer than 500 calories a day when a normal, healthy person my size needed 1500–2000 per day?

On this morning however, I tended obediently to my port after my infusion. Standing over the kitchen sink, I washed my hands thoroughly, pulled down the scoop-neck collar of my pajama top and unscrewed the TPN tubing. With an alcohol swab, I wiped the nozzle, counting to fifteen to make sure it was sterile. Then I quickly attached a plastic syringe filled with ten milliliters of saline and flushed it slowly. Once that was empty, I did the same with a second syringe filled with five milliliters of heparin, to prevent blood clots. Business as usual. As I got ready to clean up, I suddenly felt like someone was holding a blowtorch to my head. The heat blinded me and I lost my balance. My chest tightened and a sharp pain stabbed my heart. I couldn't breathe! I opened my mouth to get air, but couldn't inhale. What was happening? This was not one of my usual fainting spells.

Don was still out walking the dogs, so even if I could've called out to him, he wouldn't have heard me. I stumbled into the living room and fell onto the couch. *Am I having a heart attack? Am I dying?* As my shoulder hit the cushion I felt Henry's warm little body near my face. Then I felt his small pink tongue rapidly licking my lips and nose. I was not alone. My panic subsided a bit and I realized that I had taken a breath. *Can I trust that my one remaining lung will take in more air or am I going to suffocate?*

Henry barked to get my attention. My breathing instincts kicked in and I put my hand on the top of his head to let him know that I was okay. At least I could breathe. What had just happened? Henry climbed onto my chest and put his face on my neck. His wet little nose felt cool. I wrapped my left arm around him and gratefully drew another breath.

"Thank you, Henry. Thank you, thank you, and thank you." He had put himself on duty without any command from me. What a good boy. His impressive response to my spell helped reduce my fear of dying in the moment. Resting on the couch seemed like the wisest thing to do, so I stayed still, appreciating every breath I took in. Don would be home with Arty and Dixie soon.

Through the window I heard the jingle-jangle of dog collars. Don and the big brown dogs were back from their walk. The front door opened, and the two big dogs came running in with Don a few steps behind. He saw me lying on the couch, an unusual place for me to be at eight in the morning.

"Are you okay?" he asked calmly.

"I think so."

"What's wrong?" He came closer, looking concerned.

"I don't know what just happened, but right after I flushed my port, I had a horrible chest pain and couldn't breathe. I've never been so scared in my life, but Henry was right there," I boasted. "He put himself on duty and licked my face! I couldn't believe it. He wasn't even in the room when I started feeling bad."

"Good boy, buddy. Do we need to take you to the ER, sweetie?" Don sat down next to me.

"No, I think it passed, but I'll call Dr. Teddy Bear this morning and see what I should do. Henry really did his job. I'm so proud of him. Good boy, Henry!"

"Are you sure you're okay?" Don asked again.

"Yeah, I think so. I'm just going to lie here for a while. God, I'm exhausted all a sudden."

"Do you need anything? Some water?"

"Yeah, that sounds good. I just want to sleep."

In the sixteen years that Don and I had been together, this was not the first time he had seen me in crisis. He was concerned but remained calm.

After resting on the couch for an hour with Henry, I called Dr. Teddy Bear. He was not in, but once I told the nurse what had happened she insisted that I come in right away to see his colleague, Dr. Thomas.

Don drove me to his office and I told him what happened.

"What you're describing sounds like a pulmonary embolism," Dr. Thomas said. "In most cases, a pulmonary embolism is caused by a blood clot that travels to the lungs from another part of the body, most commonly the legs."

"Do you think that's what happened to me?" I asked.

"In your case a piece of the clot could have broken off while you were flushing the port with the saline or Heparin, sending a particle into your lung, which would stop your breathing. I'm sending you for a CT scan. That will show if there is a clot somewhere that's shedding. Hopefully, if there was a small piece of something, it has broken apart and you'll never hear from it again."

"That's pretty scary," I said.

"Promise me you'll go straight to the emergency room next time you experience difficulty breathing, chest pains, or a racing heart," he insisted.

"I will. I promise." I meant what I said, because the intense fear I had experienced that morning was fresh in my mind. My familiarity with emergency rooms had grown in recent years as my health problems had increased, so I was not shy about using them.

Dr. Thomas ordered a bunch of tests, including the CT angiogram. He was nice and proactive, and even though he was not Dr. Teddy Bear, I trusted him.

Coping with all my physical and emotional health issues made me familiar with many ways to get help, including doctors, hospitals, therapy, prayer, meditation, yoga, and even knitting with friends. My gratitude was huge for all these, but on the morning that Henry rose to the occasion to keep me conscious during my pulmonary embolism, I gained a new appreciation for the therapeutic benefits of dogs. Even though Henry had completed six months of training and passed his test, it wasn't until that morning that I truly believed he could be so extraordinarily helpful. He had proved himself. It would not be the last time.

CHAPTER 11

Explaining Henry

"YOU CAN'T BRING YOUR dog to work," scolded a senior staff member as I walked from my office to the main administrative building. Her words pierced me like arrows. This was only Henry's third day at work, and I still felt timid about walking around the zoo with him, but I had to go to the mail room. I respected this woman. She was one of the zoo's main animal curators, but her seniority intimidated me. Did she really think that I had the audacity to bring a pet to work?

"This is Henry, he's my service dog," I faltered. "He's fully trained, and all his paperwork is on file in Human Resources."

"But he's so small. How can he possibly help you?" she asked, looking a bit confused. My knees were shaking and I was choked up, so there was no way I was going to explain how he helped me. I kept walking as if nothing was wrong. I knew my rights, but buckled when I had to defend them.

Before taking ten steps, I encountered another employee who was not quite as high on the food chain as the senior staffer, but just as imposing. "You can't bring your dog to work with you," she informed me, as if she couldn't believe I would do such a thing.

"He's my service dog," I said, choking back tears and attempting to defend myself for the second time.

"Oh really?" she asked, sounding genuinely curious now. "What's the matter? I mean, why do you need him?" *What a bitch.*

"I'd rather not discuss my medical problems. He supports me," I said, realizing that this was the first time she had spoken to me since I started working at the zoo.

"Really?" she asked again. "That's fascinating." Her tone softened, and she seemed to recognize that she had crossed a delicate and dangerous line. Determined to complete my task of retrieving the mail, I kept walking, but my steps got heavier and heavier as I unraveled.

"Hi, Henry!" a cheerful voice called as I entered the little mailroom. It was Kai from HR. What a relief.

"How are you?" she asked me.

"Not so good," I couldn't hide my tears.

"What's wrong, dear?" Her concern was genuine so I explained my two recent encounters with employees.

"I know they were just doing their jobs by asking about Henry, but it hurt," I confided in her.

"I'm so sorry. I will inform them that they have been inappropriate. I will let them know that there is a correct way to address someone with a dog on zoo grounds. If they think the dog is a pet, they need to *ask* about the dog's status, not scold the person without knowing the situation."

"Thanks, Kai." Her words comforted me for the moment, and I could return to my office and finish my work for the day.

However, the next morning, as I was preparing to go to work, all I could think about was people interrogating me about Henry. I got dizzy and had to lie down.

"What's wrong, honey?" Don asked when he saw me on the couch.

"I'm okay. I just don't want to be yelled at anymore by people who don't know what they're talking about!"

"Who cares what they think?" Don didn't care what others thought of him. Why couldn't I be more like him?

"I know, but now I'm so anxious I can't even think straight. It's exhausting trying to defend myself all the time."

"So call in sick," Don suggested.

"I can't miss work."

"Why not? Give yourself a break from those assholes."

"You're right." I called in sick.

***

When I excitedly embarked on a life enhanced by a service dog, I anticipated many hours, days and months of training, as well as a lot of anxiety before passing the certification exams. What I did not anticipate were all the other challenges that came with having a four-footed assistant by my side. To begin with, I never imagined that Henry would attract so much attention. How could I have thought that I would be unnoticed as I walked around in public with a super-cute, ten-pound chihuahua/dachshund in a tiny, orange service dog vest? Was it ignorance, optimism, or oblivion that prevented me from anticipating the pain of scrutiny that Henry's presence would generate?

In the big, open room where I worked, Henry hung out in the little dog bed I had set up for him under my desk. He was not visible to the volunteers when they came to sign in at the computer, which was a good thing, because it protected me from being bombarded with inquiries about him. In my weekly newsletter to our volunteers, I introduced Henry and explained that he was not a pet, he was on duty, and people should not address him or try to pet him. Keeping people from talking to Henry would be a challenge, because the one thing all our volunteers had in common was their love for animals.

"Good morning!" Gladys, one of our grandmotherly volunteers greeted me on one of Henry's first days in the office. "I heard about your dog; can I meet him?" She started to come behind my desk to get a closer look.

"Sure," I gathered up all my willingness and courtesy and prepared to be uncomfortable. "May I ask that you step back and let me put him in a down-stay? Then I can release him so he can say hello."

"Yes, of course," she replied and curbed her desire to get in close.

"Henry, heel," I patted my right leg and guided him on my left side to sit. "Henry, down." He obediently obliged. "This is Henry. Henry, this is Gladys."

"Oh, he is sooo cute! May I pet him?"

"Yeah, but first I have to release him. Henry, stay," I said, holding my left hand down to guide him. "Good boy . . . Okay!"

At this command, he knew he could get out of his down-stay and go to Gladys. He loved people, especially kind, older ladies who welcomed him with ear scratches and belly rubs. He ran to her. "Good boy, Henry."

"What does he do for you?" Gladys asked. In that moment, I could see that she was just curious. She was not judging or scrutinizing me in any way. And yet it still sounded like she was asking "What's wrong with you?"

"He helps me when I feel faint," I shared.

"Do you feel faint a lot?" She sounded more concerned than judgmental.

"Yeah. More than I like."

"But what does he do when that happens?" she pushed. This was just the beginning of many months of invasive questioning I would have to deal with.

"He is trained to get on my chest if I actually go down and lick my face aggressively. It's called 'tactile stimulation.' It's like having water splashed on your face." This response would be fine-tuned over the next few months when I answered questions from many of our volunteers.

"That's amazing," Gladys said, in total awe of Henry's skill. Henry grew tired of being petted and put himself back on his little dog bed under my desk. "Okay, bye-bye, Henry. Thanks for letting me meet him."

"You're welcome. Thank you for coming to see us." Once Gladys was gone, I relaxed and realized that our encounters with the volunteers may not be so awkward after all. There was no need for me to tell them how he helped me with my anorexia and depression. Giving people a response about my physical problems satisfied them, and that was all I needed to do.

The law protected my privacy regarding my diagnosis, so I was not obligated to tell anyone, not even my employers, why I needed Henry. But I did need to make people aware of the duties he performed in the event that something happened to me and he tried to communicate with them. My coworkers needed to know his signals so they could respond.

If a staff member, volunteer, or zoo guest sounded critical or skeptical when asking about Henry or me I would give them a quick, cold "Oh, I don't want to bore you with all my medical complications. He helps me." Period, end of conversation. Nobody needed to know any more than that. Then I'd smile and walk away to keep them from knowing how insecure I really was.

Henry learned quickly that he liked to go to work with me. In the mornings as I got ready, he looked at me with such great enthusiasm that I found myself eager to get to work too. His cute little face said, "Come on, Mommy, let's go have some fun!" His charm quickly earned him many fans. Many of these fans were the women with whom I worked, and they fondly referred to him as "the Chick Magnet." As I walked through the office, people heard the jingling of his dog tags and rushed out from behind their cubicle walls to see their little four-legged boyfriend.

"Hi, Henry! Oh, I'm sorry; I should ask if I can pet him. Can he go on a break?" begged a female coworker. Because she was respectful enough to ask permission, my heart softened, and I decided in the moment that Henry deserved a break. I released him from duty by putting him in a down-stay, got his attention and said "Okay!" At this point he jumped out of his position and eagerly approached his friend to be petted and hopefully get a biscuit. The experience of opening my heart to fellow staff members and volunteers when Henry paved the way felt good.

Henry's introduction to the world was female-centric, since many of my contacts at the zoo were women. When he met men, his reaction was more unpredictable. Sometimes he accepted them and behaved in the same loving manner as he did with women, but other times his back got rigid, which suggested that he was scared of them. He even let out warning growls and little barks as though he was protecting me from them. Weeks passed at work when this did not occur and I often forgot that he didn't adore everyone. When he emitted protective murmurs, anyone who happened to be around typically said, "Wow, I've never heard Henry bark or growl!"

"I'm sorry," I would say, feeling embarrassed by his outbursts. "I think he was just startled." In many cases, he was simply surprised by the sudden noise of the door opening, and I assured the person that Henry's vocalizations were not a personal attack, nor did they reflect how he felt about them. That said, there was one individual on staff that Henry was unmistakably wary of.

***

Before Henry appeared on the scene, I had established healthy, professional working relationships with all my coworkers at the zoo. My timidity and people-pleasing tendencies lent themselves to mutually respectful communication in most situations. To avoid conflict, I always took the coward's way out, meaning I never challenged or disagreed with any of my colleagues. Because I played so well with others, on the rare occasion when I did feel disdain for someone, I got confused and felt guilty.

But when I received an email announcing that a certain male coworker had resigned, I did a little happy dance. Actually, it was a big happy dance. Heck, it was a Broadway musical show-stopping extravaganza, I was so happy.

Mr. IT Guy was a tall, slender, dark-eyed man with a chronic scowl. His skinny neck and close-cropped, dark hair accentuated the severity of his angry face. Quite honestly, he resembled Lucifer. He moved stealthily from office to office, brilliantly troubleshooting computer problems.

"I'm so sorry. I hate to cause you so much trouble. I didn't mean to break my computer. I wasn't doing anything weird, honest," I sputtered in defense when he came to my desk. The stern expression on his face compelled me to apologize for breathing air and taking up space. Why did he always look so pissed off? Why did I blame myself for this?

"Uh huh . . . " He muttered as his fingers danced nimbly on my keyboard. He made no eye contact with me, so I was convinced he hated me. Since he had a permanent scowl, I should've known better, but my low self-esteem took me deep into embarrassment, and I felt obliged to apologize repeatedly.

He said nothing in response to my babbling. He just furrowed his brow and hastened his angry movement. My apologies pissed him off more. I couldn't win with him. Whenever he repaired my computer I always sent a "thank-you" email, because it seemed like the polite thing to do, and I usually repeated my humble apologies. After one such email he told Erin that he wanted me to stop saying, "I'm sorry," "Thank you," and "Please" when he helped me out. Later I learned that I was not the only person who angered him with common courtesy. He asked several people to stop thanking him. What a weirdo.

When Mr. IT Guy came to my office to fix something that ended up being something simple, like a loose cable, he made no effort to conceal his feelings of disdain for my ineptitude. He was a man of few words, but the one message I clearly got from his body language was that he thought I was a moron.

When Henry came on board, I hoped that his presence would soften Mr. IT Guy's jagged edges as it had with some other bristly staff members. No such luck. The first time he entered our office after Henry started coming to work with me Henry let out a piercing howl that I had never heard before. His startling vocalization came out before he even laid eyes on Mr. IT Guy. My face flushed from embarrassment, and I was terrified that Henry's barking would reveal how uncomfortable I was in Mr. IT Guy's presence.

"Henry! Halt," I instructed him, but a big part of me wanted to let Henry off his leash to snarl and scare this mean monster out of the room. Henry's growling gave a voice to my feelings and protected me at the same time. *Good boy Henry, get 'im!*

Mr. IT Guy just rolled his eyes and walked away without comment.

After Henry's initial reaction to him, I made a genuine effort to prevent him from snarling when Mr. IT Guy entered the room. Eventually Henry understood and mostly stopped his howling, but his instincts were on the money.

Every year in June, the zoo had a huge evening fundraising event, and I helped the guests check in at the front gates. The crowds and chaos made me anxious, and even though I could have benefitted from Henry's calming presence, I worried that he would attract too much attention from the patrons as they arrived and consequently make us both anxious. So I chose to leave him home for the evening.

"Where's Henry?" one of our female volunteers asked.

"I gave him the night off because he'd spend the whole evening trying to get me out of the madding crowds." I kept my tone jocular, but it was true. Henry always sensed when I was uncomfortable in big groups and tried to pull me to a quieter venue.

Out of nowhere, Mr. IT Guy appeared behind me to plug in some wires.

"Hi," I said, attempting to be civil, knowing full well I was asking for trouble by engaging him in conversation.

"Hi, Martha," he responded without making eye contact. "Where's your buddy?"

"I gave him the night off. He doesn't like parties," I said, trying to stay lighthearted.

"Don't you take him to big public spaces?" he asked, sounding very critical.

"No, they make him uncomfortable." I stopped there because I knew that anything more than short sentences irritated him.

"That's interesting." His simple reply was loaded with meaning. *He's questioning whether or not Henry is a proper service dog.* Our conversation came to an awkward end, and I walked away with my tail between my legs. *Ouch.* If someone else had said the exact same thing, it would not have upset me, but Mr. IT Guy's tone was accusatory. If anyone else had asked about Henry, I would have been happy to explain how he helped me. I would have been happy to explain that he had strengths and weaknesses. *Why do I care so much what Mr. IT Guy thinks of me?*

For the next three days, I could not get those two words out of my head. *"That's interesting... that's interesting . . . that's interesting . . . "* The dreams I had after that were filled with strangers saying things like, *"That's interesting . . . so Henry is as much of a fraud as you are. Who do you think you are fooling with your nice-girl act? Everyone knows you're a nut case. Mr. IT Guy has read all your emails. You know he has access to all the Google searches you make about mental illness, medications, and all the other incriminating topics you research. You can't hide. Everyone knows you're a fruitcake and Henry is just a dumb dog."*

Actually, I was a fraud at work because I constantly tried to convince people that I was a healthy, happy, sane person. Of course Mr. IT Guy was not the cause of my insecurities or my self-doubt, but after he resigned, the voices in my head temporarily quieted down.

CHAPTER 12

Knowledge Is Power

ON ONE LEVEL, I knew my efforts to train and use a service dog were novel and gutsy, and I had every right to be proud of Henry and myself. On another level, I was overwhelmed by the responsibility I had taken on. *What were you thinking? Where did you get the idea that you had the courage to break ground and be the first zoo employee to have a service dog?* How could I have known that curious people would innocently invade my privacy with their inquiries and mean-spirited people would challenge me about his presence?

Common sense told me there were other people in the world who faced similar problems, so using the words "challenges of having a service dog," I searched the Internet and found an organization called Service Dog Central, a community of service dog partners and trainers who shared a lot of helpful information.[3]

The website said that, according to the University of Arizona, 0.9% of people with disabilities were partnered with service dogs, which worked out to approximately 15,000 pups across the U.S. The site also featured information on training, handling, access issues, rights and legal issues, public education, advocating, and support for people like me.

I was especially happy to find advice on the Service Dog Central website on how to respond to ignorant questions.[4] For example, when challenged by a business owner who clearly did not know that the law permitted service dogs in stores, one could respond in a friendly, confident way by stating their rights, thereby educating the owner. This was much more effective than getting defensive, or my response, which was getting embarrassed, bursting into tears and running out of the store. The website also suggested carrying little cards with the law printed on one side and the name of one's service dog on the other, which one could hand to people when challenged.

Another website, ServicePoodle.org, specifically addressed some of the issues I was facing.[5] Maeve, a standard poodle service dog, was the site's "spokesperson": the photos of her sweet face made the website very appealing. She and her owner advocated for people like me, who were new to the service dog world and easily intimidated. Maeve provided the following list of the "cons of having a service dog."

1. If your disability was not apparent before you got a service dog, it will be after you do so. Even if it was apparent, you'll be spotted sooner and get more attention with a service dog. (However, access will get easier over time and as local businesses begin to recognize you).

2. You WILL be challenged about your dog frequently when you enter premises where pets are not allowed.

3. You will be challenged by a law enforcement officer at some point. Chances are good that he or she won't do so entirely appropriately.

4. Your disability will be discussed on or before the first date if you are single and have a service dog.

5. Some people will pay more attention to the dog than to you.

6. Every public errand takes much longer with a service dog.

7. People may assume you are training the dog for someone else.

8. Stress on relationships is increased.

9. Even the best-trained dog will eventually do something embarrassing in public.

Seeing these stumbling blocks in print, written by a disabled person like myself, gave me great comfort. I was not alone. Reading them also made me laugh, because they were so accurate.

The most informative, reassuring organization I found, which addressed nearly all my fears, was the International Association of Assistance Dog Partners, IAADP. Their website stated that they were "A nonprofit, cross-disability organization representing people partnered with guide, hearing and service dogs."[6]

IAADP's mission was to (1) provide assistance dog partners with a voice in the assistance dog field; (2) enable those partnered with guide dogs, hearing dogs, and service dogs to work together on issues of mutual concern; and (3) foster the disabled person/ assistance dog partnership.

On this amazing website, I found a twenty-page document written by a woman named Joan Froling, who co-founded Sterling Service Dogs to meet the growing need of to find and train dogs with the temperament and aptitude to become capable service dogs. The document was entitled "SERVICE DOG TASKS for PSYCHIATRIC DISABILITIES, Tasks to mitigate certain disabling illnesses classified as mental impairments under The Americans with Disabilities Act."[7]

The article listed the tasks a service dog could be trained to do that would serve to mitigate the effects of a disabling condition classified as a psychiatric disability. Certain tasks were developed for those who had become disabled by panic disorder, post-traumatic stress disorder (PTSD), or depression, conditions attributed to a brain chemistry malfunction. The list also contained some activities that would be useful as coping mechanisms, but would not stand up in a court of law as "a trained task that mitigates the effect of a disability," and those would be marked with a disclaimer to provide guidance to a therapist and patient on that issue.[8]

Following the introduction, Ms. Froling's document went into great detail about disabilities and the tasks that dogs could learn to aid their person. There were four categories of assistance work or tasks for psychiatric disabilities:

I.   Assistance in a Medical Crisis
II. Treatment Related Assistance
III. Assistance Coping with Emotional Overload
IV. Security Enhancement Tasks

Reading through the detailed list of psychiatric disabilities and the tasks that service dogs learned to assist their person reassured me. When Henry and I went through training we had used the list from the ADA, but it did not embellish the emotional challenges. Part of me wanted to carry Joan Froling's detailed document with me at all times to pull out so I could show people I was not the only person finding unconventional ways to cope in the world. Doing this research gave me some courage and opened my eyes to the reality that I needed to do more to educate myself and the rest of the world.

Once I understood and accepted my new responsibility to teach people about the blessings of service dogs, I was inspired to find other people who had similar stories. Coincidently, as my fire was being fanned, my mother sent me an article from *The Wall Street Journal* called "'Sit! Stay! Snuggle!': An Iraq Vet Finds His Dog Tuesday."[9] The article described how a three-year-old golden retriever service dog named Tuesday helped Luis Carlos Montalvan, a retired Army captain and recipient of a Purple Heart for wounds he suffered in Iraq.

Mr. Montalvan suffered from severe PTSD, and his pup assisted with things like reminding him to take his daily medications, preventing panic attacks in public by presenting his calming muzzle, putting his head on Mr. Montalvan's leg or lap when he got anxious, and reassuring him that he was not alone.

Prior to getting his service dog, Mr. Montalvan's body and emotional state had rapidly deteriorated due to the injuries he'd suffered in the war as well as his PTSD. To sleep at night, he was taking a lot of medications and drinking alcohol. He lived alone in his small Brooklyn apartment, and his depression had been driving him seriously to consider suicide. Fortunately, he sought help that led to his acquiring Tuesday. Even though it took him more than four months to adjust to his dog, Mr. Montalvan was finally able to venture out into the world. Without Tuesday's help, these activities were not possible. He could go to movies, to his Veterans Administration group counseling sessions in Manhattan, and to his classes at Columbia University, where he studied journalism and communication.

Luis Carlos Montalvan was one of the fortunate disabled veterans whose life improved as the result of being paired with a service dog. Even though my disability was not the result of a nightmarish war experience, his story brightened my outlook, and I was reminded that I was not the only person in the world whose disability was not as apparent as blindness.

This same *Wall Street Journal* article mentioned a program called Puppies Behind Bars. Incarcerated canines? Dogs in jail? Memories of the ferocious packs of feral dogs that used to terrorize our neighborhood came to mind. As much as I loved dogs, the fearless ferals looked like hardened criminals loose on the streets. Fortunately, my impressions were way off base. Puppies Behind Bars was an organization that assisted in the training of service dogs for war veterans. The name was clever. It made me smile and I wanted to know more.

When I did an internet search, I found an episode of *Fresh Air* on National Public Radio. Dave Davies, senior writer for the *Philadelphia Daily News*, was talking to Gloria Gilbert Stoga, founder of the program; Nora Moran, a former prison inmate who now worked for the program; and Paul Bang-Knudsen, a former corporal in the Marine Corps. Mr. Bang-Knudsen, who was wounded in Iraq, had a service dog that had been trained by prison inmates through the PBB program.

Based on the needs of the communities in which she was working in 2006, Gloria Gilbert Stoga started raising dogs to assist disabled children and adults. She then launched an organization called "Dog Tags: Service Dogs for Those Who've Served Us," through which fully-trained service dogs were donated to wounded soldiers coming home from Iraq and Afghanistan.

The primary raisers of the dogs were prison inmates. In order to train the puppies, the inmates kept the dogs in their cells and went to Puppies Behind Bars classes once a week. Two or three weekends a month, the pups also went to "puppy-sitters" outside of the prisons in the community, who took the dogs into their homes so they could be exposed to situations they wouldn't experience in prison. The dogs needed experience with real-world sights, sounds, and smells so they wouldn't need further training once they were placed with their person. The program had over 400 volunteers in local communities who took the puppies out of prison for a couple of hours or a full weekend.

Before they were even housebroken, the dogs started living with their trainer-inmates 24/7, where a kennel was set up in each prisoner's cell. The pups learned 85 different commands, five of which were made up specifically to benefit the soldiers with PTSD and/or traumatic brain injury. Some of the primary tasks included picking up objects, opening doors, holding doors open, getting water bottles out of the refrigerator, or turning lights on and off.

The dogs learned to mitigate the startle responses of war survivors with PTSD. For example, in any big store, like a Costco or a grocery store with wide aisles, walking around a corner could be very stressful because a veteran could be startled by an unseen person approaching from the opposite direction. For someone without PTSD, the sudden confrontation might just prompt an "Excuse me," but for a damaged war veteran, this kind of surprise could lead to flashbacks of war and trigger his or her survival instinct as if the situation were a dangerous fight-or-flight moment.

One of the commands that their puppy learned to help their person while shopping was "pop the corner," which meant that he or she walked slightly ahead of the person, looked around corners and identified whether or not there was someone coming.

The pups learned how to obey commands, behave appropriately, and grow into obedient, good-natured service dogs. The raisers benefited as well. They got to enjoy the companionship of their charge and inevitably they matured as a result of having the responsibility of raising a dog for a disabled person, thereby giving back to society. Puppy-raisers supplied love and tenderness to the pups and provided the solid foundation critical in the development of a good service dog.

For sixteen months, the pups lived in prison with their trainers. At that point, the pups were tested to determine whether they were fit to go to the next stage of training, which would fully prepare them to perform as service dogs for a disabled person. Once they demonstrated suitability, PBB sent them to the special service dog schools where they continued their formal training. If the animals couldn't continue on the track to become working dogs, Puppies Behind Bars donated them to families with blind children. In either case, these puppies, raised in such a unique environment, spent their lives as companions to people who needed them.

PBB currently has programs in six prisons: Bedford Hills Correctional Facility in New York, Edna Mahan Correctional Facility in New Jersey, Federal Correctional Institution in Connecticut, Fishkill Correctional Facility in New York, Mid-Orange Correctional Facility in New York, and Otisville Correctional Facility in New York. Not surprisingly, nearly everyone in these institutions benefits from the presence of the puppies, including staff and all the other inmates.

Having felt "imprisoned" for much of my life by my various illnesses, particularly my anorexia, I identified with the inmates' experience of finding love in the company of dogs and freedom in the act of helping others.

CHAPTER 13

Dogs and More

A PLETHORA OF SCIENTIFIC data has proven animals can improve a person's health. To be a better advocate of service dogs, I did a lot of research on this topic. The National Institutes of Health (NIH), Department of Health and Human Services examined 421 adults who had had heart attacks. The scientists found that after a year, many of the people who were still alive had dogs.[10] Another NIH study looked at 240 married couples. The individuals in the group who had lower heart rates and blood pressure, at rest and when undergoing stressful tests, owned pets. The results also indicated that single patients who recovered with a pet in their homes did so faster than those who recovered with a spouse or a friend and no pet.[11]

Understandably, the dog owners in the study got more exercise on a regular basis than those without because they took their dogs on walks. One NIH-funded investigation studied over 2,000 adults and found that dog-walking owners were more active and less likely to be obese than those who didn't own or walk a dog. This study also found that older dog walkers had greater mobility as they navigated inside their homes.[12]

Social interaction, helpful in the healing stages of illness, is also enhanced by owning and caring for a dog. Anyone who has walked a dog knows that encountering other dog walkers when out for some daily exercise with their pup is inevitable. Conversations come easily when we walk our best friends. When I encounter fellow dog walkers and engage in friendly conversation, I am often embarrassed the next time I see them because I usually remember the dog's name, but rarely that of the person. Still, whether or not I remember anyone's name, my spirits are often lifted when I stop to talk to other dog walkers.

Kids can really benefit too from the assistance of dogs, especially in the development of their socialization. Dr. James Griffin, a scientist at NIH's Eunice Kennedy Shriver National Institute of Child Development, stated, "When children are asked who they talk to when they get upset, a lot of times their first answer is their pet."[13]

Pets provide a great source of comfort and they help develop empathy. The NIH reports that children with autism can learn how to interact better with people by learning how to do so with pets first.

Animal lovers don't need to be told that their pets provide healing comfort, but what many people may not realize is that through research and training, the help of animals can hugely improve the quality of life for people with all kinds of ailments.

***

The bond between animals and people is so powerful that a form of therapy called Animal-Assisted Therapy (AAT) has evolved from it. The concept of healing with the help of animals has been in place for centuries, but in the past several decades the movement has become more formal and organized.

AAT started in the late 18th century at the York Retreat in England, a facility where the patients could wander the grounds in the company of small domestic animals. According to James Serpell, professor of humane ethics amd animal welfare at University of Pennsylvania School of Veterinary Medicine, this encouraged the patients to socialize with each other and staff. [14] Half a century later the Bethlehem Hospital, which is known to us as Bedlam, added animals to their wards to boost patient morale. Bethlehem is one of the oldest mental institutions in the world. Founded by Christians in 1247 to shelter and care for the homeless, it gradually focused more on those considered "mad."[15]

Since I have been concerned about the soundness of my own mind for decades, the history of animals being used to help patients in Bedlam fascinated me.

Sigmund Freud, the founding father of psychoanalysis, kept dogs, specifically a Chow Chow named Jofi, who was present for many of his sessions. He reported that the dog's presence was reassuring to his patients, especially adolescents, and helped them to relax and confide. Not surprising.

We are most familiar with direct assistance given by "seeing-eye dogs" to visually impaired people, but other programs incorporate the benefits of a variety of animals for many disabilities and conditions. AAT treatment plans have helped combat loneliness, stress, depression, and other emotional problems. A treatment plan can be as simple as prescribing a pet at home to provide companionship. In other situations, the plan can integrate fish, birds, or rabbits into clinical situations, which enables patients to let down their guard and more fully participate in their therapy. Other animals used in treatment include dolphins, cats, cows, elephants, and horses.[16]

Equine Assisted Therapy (EAT) first came to my attention in 1998 when I went to the hospital in Florida for my anorexia. When I was there, I was befriended by a fourteen-year-old girl named Shannon, who, like her twin sister, had already been in six different hospitals for anorexia nervosa. Their minds and bodies were completely saturated by their eating disorder, just as mine had been at the age of fourteen.

Shannon excitedly shared with me her experience at another eating disorder hospital in Wickenburg, Arizona, called Ramuda Ranch.

"It was really cool. I wanna go back there," she shared.

"What was so cool about it?" I wondered.

"We got to ride horses," she said excitedly.

"No way, really?" The fourteen-year-old inside me woke up.

"Yeah, if we followed our treatment plan, ate 100% of our meals and gained weight, we got to work with them."

"What else did you do besides ride them?"

"We learned how to groom them too."

"What a great idea! I want to go there."

I immediately went online and found their website, which

states, "Ramuda Ranch, the hospital for eating disorders, has been treating eating disorders and obsessive-compulsive disorder for more than twenty years."

The Spanish word "ramuda" referred to the group of horses used to give rest and provide a fresh start for the journey ahead. As I knew too well, the process of recovering from anorexia was a rough journey. Being able to work with a horse would've been a huge help.

Various other organizations use EAT with their patients. At the Saddle Light Center in Selma, Texas, physical therapists and trained riding instructors offer horse-assisted therapy to disabled people of all ages. The Triple H Equitherapy Center in Bandera County, Texas, provides EAT to help people who have mental, emotional, and physical disabilities develop basic life skills.

The North American Riding for the Handicapped Association (NARHA) trains animal handlers and provides accreditation for those who practice this amazing therapy, and carefully select appropriate horses that have been trained specifically for this purpose.

Under the psycho-therapeutic guidance of a mental health professional and trained horse handlers, patients learn to care for a horse through grooming, feeding, and leading. Therapeutic riding teaches disabled people how to ride a horse, which can increase strength, coordination, control, balance, and orientation.

Patients with autism or Asperger's syndrome are said to be calmer and have an increased ability to focus as a result of the rhythmic motion of horse riding. Grooming and riding can improve gross motor function and reduce anxiety.

People whose disabilities diminish their ability to care for their appearance and hygiene can improve in those areas by learning to regularly groom a horse. And those with weak communication skills can gain confidence through learning to give a horse commands.

Working as the coordinator of volunteer programs at the zoo gave me the opportunity to learn first-hand about the many ways people heal with animals. Being around animal lovers, especially volunteers, who devoted themselves to educating zoo visitors out of the kindness of their hearts, I got to hear some great stories.

Our department had a wonderful outreach program that traveled to people who could not come to the zoo. Specially trained volunteers took small, live animals and other touchable items such as pelts and replicas of animal skulls to a variety of facilities: schools for children with disabilities, hospitals, daycare centers (adult and children), and nursing homes. The volunteers used a van that was uniquely equipped to transport animals off zoo grounds.

Typically, three of our older female volunteers, who had the wisdom and soft edges of grandmothers, put on their sunny yellow outreach T-shirts, collected the animals that would be going on the excursion—which included a non-venomous snake, a lizard, a guinea pig, a hedgehog, and/or a chicken—loaded up the Zoo Mobile van and hit the road. Once they got to the facility, they gave thirty-minute presentations, always tailored to the understanding abilities of their audience that day. They introduced different species and explained how the animals adapted and thrived within their natural habitat. They also explained what made the animal special, incorporating information about their native habitat, behavior, and diet. The listeners were encouraged to touch the guest animals and to ask questions.

One afternoon, our outreach volunteers came back from a retirement home and shared that a resident of the home had taken a shine to Lucy, the chicken. The elderly woman got very excited, smiled, and told the volunteers how much she liked Lucy. The volunteers were pleased, but didn't think it was out of the ordinary until a little later, when one of the nurses reported that prior to Lucy's visit, this older female resident had not uttered a word in six months. The nurses didn't really know why she had stopped talking, but because the woman was also very depressed, they were concerned. It turned out that she had owned chickens when she was younger, and Lucy brought back happy memories, giving her the courage and willingness to speak after a long silence.

During my twenties, when I was in heavy denial about my eating disorder, I would not have been able to talk about my illness or ask for help even if a gun had been held to my head. When I reached thirty and found myself slipping into a depression, triggered by frustration from my acting career, it was the presence of Gus, with his unconditional love and total dependence on me, that opened my heart and mind enough to ask for help. When I looked into Gus's root-beer-colored eyes, I knew he loved me no matter what, and that made me want to live. As a result, I was willing to try therapy for the first time in my life. Since that time, my healthiest decisions have been inspired by the love I get from my animals.

CHAPTER 14

Equal Opportunity Service Dog

ONCE I GOT THROUGH the awkward first months of being questioned about Henry's presence and my need for him, a welcome shift occurred. I started to notice that when coworkers initiated conversations with me about him, they always had big smiles on their faces. Usually when someone caught sight of Henry, they'd do a double take, probably because they were surprised to see a dog in the office, then their eyes would light up. At times their excitement was a little startling, but their energy was genuinely benevolent and they were perfectly harmless. Why hadn't I seen that before?

Most of the people on staff at the zoo liked animals, but that didn't guarantee they would like Henry or want him around, so I was very cautious when approaching individuals whom I didn't know well. For example, one of the senior staff members, a small, stringent woman named Jamie scared the daylights out of me. She had the monstrous responsibility of organizing all the zoo's major fundraising events. I'd seen her in action, barking orders at her underlings, and from what I observed, she had no soft edges and no compassion. For safety's sake, I avoided contact with her, especially when Henry came on the scene.

One afternoon I had to walk past her office to deliver some paperwork to a colleague. As we passed, I gripped Henry's leash and pulled him close.

"Hi!" she called out as I scurried by.

"Hi," I said and stopped to be polite.

"Is that Henry?" she asked.

"Yeah," I said, wishing she hadn't seen me. She dropped what she was doing, got up and went to a nearby cabinet and grabbed a bag of dog biscuits. Bag in hand, she came around to the front of her large, cluttered desk, plopped down onto the floor and started talking to Henry.

"Hi, little Henry. Do you want a cookie?" she asked in a playful voice, which I never expected out of her.

"Yes, please," I answered for Henry. "I'm sure he wants one. Henry, halt." I gave him the command so I could temporarily release him for a visit.

"Good boy. Now sit." He sat. "Good boy." His lessons were fresh in his mind and he responded obediently. "Okay, you can say hello." He sprang to his feet and ran to Jamie. His little black and tan body wiggled back and forth in anticipation of getting the snack she held. Happily, he crunched up the treat and put himself back into a "sit-stay" position, then stared into Jamie's eyes, hoping for another one. "Good boy, Henry," we both praised him.

"You are so precious, little Henry. I don't usually like small dogs, but you're special. You're like a big dog in a tiny body," our new friend Jamie said. He was as smitten with her as she was with him. He rolled onto his back for a belly rub, and then bounced back up for more biscuits, which he promptly received. My cheeks started to ache from smiling. Seeing the interaction between Henry and Jamie warmed my heart. The brightness in her eyes reflected the positive impact he had on her. Seeing her drop all her defenses and melt into a dog-loving child made me see this fireball of a woman in a softer light.

A few days later, I told Erin about my unexpected experience with Jamie. In confidence, Erin then shared with me that Jamie suffered from multiple sclerosis. Not knowing what it was exactly, I did a Google search and learned that MS made the body's immune system eat the protective sheath that covered the nerves. It messed up the communication between the brain and the rest of the body and permanently wrecked nerves. Even though Jamie had this awful illness that must have caused a lot of physical and emotional problems, she didn't appear to feel sorry for herself. When I witnessed Henry's positive impact on her, I realized that his presence would be therapeutic not just for me, but for my coworkers as well, and that made me very happy.

The following week, when we passed by Jamie's office, Henry tugged at his leash to go in.

"Is that little Henry?" Jamie called out.

"Hi, Jamie."

"Can he have a snack?" Jamie asked and jumped up from her desk.

"Yes, of course." I released him from duty and let him run to Jamie to get his treat. She spent the next ten minutes talking to Henry and giving him biscuits. I wasn't sure how to contribute to the conversation, but Jamie didn't care because she was enjoying Henry's affection.

"Henry, you can come visit me anytime and I'll give you cookies," she promised.

"We will definitely come back. Henry is an equal-opportunity service dog. He's available for visits if you are having a bad day, aren't you, Henry?" I said, flattered that she had invited us in again. He wagged his tail and wiggled.

"Bye, Henry. Thanks for stopping by," Jamie called out as we went about our business.

In a staff meeting a few weeks after Jamie met Henry, she shared her feelings about him with the group. "We love Henry, not only because he's so lovable, but because he helps Martha, and we want to keep her around." When my self-consciousness flared with respect to Henry's role in my life, I tried to remember her comment.

As Henry met more staff members, most of whom were women, they fell in love with him. I could see that they, too, benefitted from Henry's visits. He and I had the opportunity to lift peoples' spirits every day, and as a result, I gained friends and felt more accepted.

Every morning when I got out his little service dog vest, he'd run in circles so excitedly I could barely get him dressed. When

I opened the back door to get to the car, he'd eagerly race out, then wait for me to put him in his crate. Once we got to the zoo, he'd jump out of the car and prance proudly through the parking lot to get to my office, where he curled up on the little faux-fleece bed under my desk. He appeared to be sleeping, but in a heartbeat, or lack thereof, he'd jump up to assist me.

My self-confidence as the owner of a service dog grew over time, thanks to the positive experiences I had with some of my coworkers and volunteers.

***

"Hola, Martita," Mercedes called out as she came into our office to clean. Henry let out a loud howl.

"Hola, Mercedes," I said in my limited Spanish. "Henry! Hush up. Mind your manners. I'm sorry, Mercedes. Henry says 'Hi.' He's just being rude. Henry, shhhh!"

"Is okay," Mercedes replied with a big smile on her face. "Como estas, Martita?" she asked and reached out her arms to hug me. I loved her hugs. Several years earlier she spontaneously started hugging me whenever she came in to empty the wastebaskets. Her hugs were strong and sincere, but because she didn't speak English, I was never quite sure what she was thinking. I didn't need to know, though, since I was pretty sure I knew what she was feeling.

"I'm fine. How are *you?*" I said, returning her hug.

"Ine fine." Her lack of English and my lack of Spanish never kept us from exchanging love and affection when she came into the office to clean. Most Sundays, she came with two coworkers: David, a polite young man who spoke a little more English, and Marta, a round, little woman with a perpetual smile. I was always happy to see them because they looked happy to see me.

Mercedes, David, and Marta were three of my favorite people at the zoo. Long before Henry came onto the scene, they had won my heart with their consistent cheerfulness; consequently, I never felt intimidated by them. Beyond my fondness for them, I also felt protective of them because I had witnessed, on numerous occasions, employees of the zoo barely acknowledging their presence as they collected the garbage and swept around their desks. Mercedes, David, and Marta worked so hard and were always very polite and respectful of me. Even though I didn't speak Spanish, I made sure they knew that I appreciated them as coworkers and friends.

When Henry started coming to work with me my bond with the three of them went to a new level. Every Sunday morning he'd let out a loud howl the minute they entered the room, and would not let them approach my desk to empty my trash. He growled and barked to keep them away, which made me feel terrible because I didn't want them to feel unwelcome. After hushing Henry, I grabbed my wastebasket and took it to them so they wouldn't have to negotiate Henry's territory.

"I'm sorry. I think he's afraid of your broom, or maybe the big, plastic bags."

"Is okay," Mercedes assured me. I didn't want any of them to think that Henry's bratty barking reflected how I felt about them. Since I couldn't explain my feelings with words, I made sure they knew I appreciated them by inviting them to sit down at the big tables in the middle of the room and take a break. I brought out bottles of cold water from a little refrigerator in Erin's office, and cookies for them to snack on. When they accepted and sat down, I was honored and pleased.

Once they were sitting, without their bags and brooms, I walked Henry out from under my desk to meet them. My hunch was right: he was not barking at them. He was afraid of the noise from their brooms and bags. David offered his hand to Henry, who gently approached him and licked his fingers. Then Henry rolled over and let David rub his belly. We all laughed. They finished their snacks and went about their day. Every Sunday after that, when they came by, I had cold water and snacks ready for them.

The bond that grew between us was another pleasant surprise. Unlike other people to whom I got close because of Henry's doggy charisma, with my three custodial friends it was my need to get their forgiveness for Henry's naughty behavior that opened the door to deeper friendship. They were not offended by Henry's fear. They forgave him for howling and understood that both Henry and I were very fond of them. Every Sunday, Henry barked and I got friendly smiles and big, warm hugs.

***

Henry also had a knack for dissolving cultural barriers. Once a week, I had an appointment at an infusion and chemotherapy center to get the needle in my Port-a-Cath changed. The nurses also drew blood from my catheter, so the doctor could monitor how my body was tolerating the TPN I infused every night.

My nurses, Marion and Ellen, loved Henry, and he loved them. Marion was a strong, solid woman who spoke with an unmistakable German accent that evoked fond memories of my maternal grandfather. Her practical, hardworking approach to things was familiar to me. She was not warm and fuzzy, but she provided consistent, stellar nursing care that put my mind at ease. Ellen had a very similar demeanor, but with a Filipina flair.

Every week, when Henry and I walked in the door of the infusion center, Marion and Ellen broke out in smiles and greeted us with merriment. Their warm welcome was inspired by Henry, not me, and that was okay with me. Of course, I hoped they were happy to see me as well, but my ego didn't need to be stroked by that much enthusiasm. In fact, to be greeted with so much hoopla would've felt freakish. Henry basked in the attention, yet remained humble. He was as happy to see Marion and Ellen as they were to see him.

When I first got Henry, I hadn't even considered taking him with me to the infusion center, because I didn't think he'd be permitted. What if the other patients complained? But when I shared with Marion and Ellen how proud I was when Henry passed his tests and earned his certification, they insisted that I bring him along.

The very first time I walked through the doors of the center with Henry, each of the weary patients, who were hooked up to tubes and pumps, sitting in infusion chairs and receiving their chemotherapy, brightened up. Many of the patients were older Armenian or Mexican people who did not speak English, but the lack of a common language didn't matter. Once they saw Henry, their eyes widened, color returned to their pale, sad faces, and they called out to him in languages I couldn't understand. We didn't need to understand each other's words when Henry was around. When he bounced in, everyone knew he was fluent in friendliness and love. Gaps of culture or age vanished and we were all just patients in the infusion center. This made me smile, too.

My appreciation of Armenian baked goods also improved thanks to Henry. We were both delighted by the treats given to us by the family members of the patients we saw each week. Kurabia, a yummy butter cookie, was a favorite, as was nazook, a sweet pastry. They were both relatively bland, which my intestines appreciated, but quite tasty.

When I could share Henry's healing energy with others, whether the person was a stressed-out coworker or an elderly Armenian man in the final weeks of his battle with cancer, I knew that my union with Henry had a bigger purpose than I had previously imagined.

***

"May I pet your dog?" a very pregnant lady with bright blue eyes asked. It was the third Thursday of the month, my IVIG day, when I sat in a chair at the infusion center for four hours to get my IV immunoglobulin. My nurses were busy with other patients so I waited patiently in the little waiting area where friends and families of patients could sit, read magazines and drink coffee. The very pregnant lady introduced herself as Rosa and shared that she was waiting for her boss, an older gentleman, who was receiving his chemotherapy.

"Sure, let me release him first," I said, putting Henry in a down-stay position. "Henry, down. Good boy. Okay! You can say hello." Once released, Henry wiggled to his new friend, Rosa.

"Is he an EMS dog?" she asked.

"He's trained to help me when I feel faint," I shared, having no idea what *EMS* meant.

"I had a service dog for fourteen years. Max was a seizure alert dog because I have epilepsy. Before Max, I had his father, who was also a service dog. Max could sense that I was going to have a seizure thirty minutes before it happened, and his dad knew forty-five minutes before."

"That's so cool." Rosa's story lifted my exhausted, deflated spirits. Before meeting Rosa that morning I was feeling blue, most likely because my body was depleted from a bad flare of colitis.

"This is the first time in fourteen years I've been without a service dog," Rosa shared.

"What happened to him?" I asked carefully.

"He died last year," she said calmly.

"I'm sorry. Are you going to get another one?"

"I'm going to train another one myself, but I want to find a breed that can detect seizures and also guard my sheep. We have chickens and sheep at home."

Her story was getting better by the minute, and I felt a kinship growing between us.

"I have to wait until the baby is six months old," she said placing her left hand under her big belly. "The dog has to know that the baby is dominant, and when the baby is six months old the dog will recognize that. Then I can start training a new dog. Being without one is hard."

"Thank you for sharing that with me," I sighed. "It's nice to meet someone who understands what it's like to have a service dog."

"Yeah, I understand. Like when people say, 'You're not blind, why do you have a guide dog?'"

"Exactly! I hate when people ask, 'What's wrong with you? You don't look sick,' or 'What does the dog do for you?'"

"I know, I know," she said supportively.

Marion called to me, "Okay, Martha and Henry, we're ready for you."

"We're coming." I turned to Rosa. "Thanks for telling me your story. Good luck with everything!"

The benefits of Henry were plentiful, but there were still times I struggled with the stigma that came with having a service dog. So meeting Rosa, who knew personally what it was like, made me feel less alone.

My monthly IVIG infusion took four hours so I always brought plenty of things to keep me busy, like my knitting, a good book, my mp3 player, and paper and pen for writing. On this day, I'd also brought a newspaper article Don had cut out for me about a fifty-one-year-old woman who had a service dog who was part chihuahua like Henry.[17] His name was Steinbeck, and I wondered if he was named after a writer, as Henry had been. The article was accompanied by a great photo of the owner, Keris Myrick, holding Steinbeck up in front of her. They were looking into each other's eyes, and the scene reminded me of how Henry and I looked at each other.

Keris Myrick suffered for many years with schizo-affective disorder. In the article, she described voices in her head that told her all the cereal boxes in the grocery store were poisonous and were going to kill her. While she was standing in the aisle of the store, she was so disturbed by the voices that she angrily threw all the boxes onto the floor, making a huge mess. Afterwards, she realized what she had done and ran out of the store, scared and embarrassed. These same voices repeatedly drove her into psychiatric hospitals and into the back seats of police cars in handcuffs.

After years of treatment and courageous effort, she was able to keep the voices under control. She went back to college at Temple University in Philadelphia, and earned a bachelor's and two master's degrees. She admitted that throughout her years of education and in her early jobs, she kept her illness hidden. That all sounded very familiar.

After losing her job as a college admissions representative for yelling at a prospective student, she realized, "I needed to move onto something else where I could fully be me and not have to hide me." She found the National Alliance on Mental Illnes—NAMI—the nation's largest grassroots mental health organization, where she could become a peer mentor to people who were suffering like she had. In 2008, she was offered a job as chief executive at a company called Project Return Peer Support Network in the city of Commerce, California.

Myrick's intelligence and charisma helped her succeed, the article went on to say, but she would always be challenged by her disease, which caused delusions and depression. She consulted regularly with a psychiatrist and had learned to quiet her mind by hiding in her walk-in closet or bathroom during periods of agitation. To keep her stressors from throwing her overboard emotionally, she turned to her service dog, Steinbeck, who knew to curl up next to her when she cried.

"All I have to do is just pick him up and pet him," she said. "It's a nice distraction."

Although our diagnoses were different, I was comforted

by Myrick's story and the importance of her service dog to her day-to-day survival. Her story reinforced that I didn't have to be ashamed of the fact that one of the many services that Henry provided was psychiatric support.

A peaceful feeling came over me as I finished reading the article. My day was getting better and better. First I met Rosa, who really understood what it was like to have a service dog for an unseen disability, then I read about Keris Myrick's success using her dog Steinbeck to cope with mental illness. Having Henry in my lap made the moment perfect and I could fall into a deep sleep as I received the rest of my IVIG.

CHAPTER 15

Hagatha

BEING AT EASE WITH Henry coming to work with me took time, but because I loved my job so much, it was worth the effort. My years at the zoo, first as a volunteer, then as an employee, gave me a sense of purpose and rescued me from the oblivion of depression. As an employee in the volunteer department, my love for the zoo had evolved. My fondness for animals brought me there in the first place, then a nurturing relationship with my boss, Erin, kept me there. But after ten years I found myself disillusioned and depleted, dreading it, even with an abundance of animal therapy available to me. That's when I knew something was deeply wrong.

Even with Henry's help, my body had deteriorated to seventy-four pounds, and my diarrhea was so bad I had to wear diapers. At the same time, I started having mood swings every day that went from euphoria to desolation, and I worried I was losing my mind.

Coping with the simplest of conflicts at work, even something as basic as two volunteers talking to me at the same time, unhinged me. When I had a truly difficult task, such as disciplining a volunteer who had rudely offended a patron, I was full of self-doubt. Interacting with the many volunteers whom I coordinated came naturally, because I found great satisfaction in helping people find a home at the zoo. However, dealing with all the different personalities was challenging.

One volunteer, whom I called Hagatha, sent out red flags from the day she appeared at one of our orientations for prospective volunteers. Framing her creased visage was a crooked, brunette, ratty wig, styled in a long bob. When I sat down to interview her, I was spooked by how hollow and glassy her eyes were.

Her paperwork indicated that she was fifty-four years old, but the weathered texture of her skin suggested that she was pushing seventy. In spite of her years, she spoke in a high-pitched, child-like voice, which sounded contrived.

During her orientation interview, her syrupy sweet talk distracted me from her oddness.

"The zoo is my favorite place in the whole world, and all the people who work here are so smart and nice." Her flattery sounded disingenuous, but it made me feel good.

"We're happy you're here and grateful for your help." With the hope of nurturing her positive attitude, I gave her an assignment in our petting zoo, where she would assist the guests as they came in to visit the goats and sheep.

After Hagatha's first day in the petting zoo, she came to my office and raved about how much she loved it and how happy she was going to be there. "Everyone was so nice, and I could tell that the goats loved me." From under my desk, Henry let out a little growl.

"Henry, be nice," I scolded him, a little embarrassed that he was expressing a warning. "I'm sorry, sometimes he gets nervous when people get close to my desk." I knew he was responding to her eerie energy, but I didn't want her to know what I was thinking.

"That's okay. Hi, Henry!" Hagatha said.

Henry growled back.

"I know he loves me. All animals love me."

"I'm glad you had such a good day in the petting zoo," I encouraged her, even though she was trying a little too hard to convince me that everything was peaches and cream.

"See you next week," she called out as she left the office.

"Bye, thanks again," I answered.

Within two weeks of her starting in the petting zoo, the head keeper left me a voicemail insisting that Hagatha be permanently dismissed from her post because she had been bossy and rude to the patrons. I never needed to address that issue, because the very next weekend she came to me asking for a different assignment.

"What other job can I try? The petting zoo is fine, but I want to try something else." She made no mention of the friction she had caused in the petting zoo. To avoid humiliating her, I didn't bring up the head keeper's remarks.

I suggested she help with our enrichment department. This amazing team of staff and volunteers enhanced the environments of our zoo residents with mental and physical stimulation that encouraged natural, healthy behavior. In other words, they gave them toys and challenges to make their lives fun. Staffers guided volunteers to help create feeder devices such as burlap bags filled with hay and treats, and small, hollow logs filled with fruit and raisins. The enrichment team also applied scents, such as spices, food, perfume, and dung around an exhibit to stimulate the animals.

Hagatha liked the sound of working with the enrichment team and attended a couple of Saturday workshops. Again, we received a negative report about her from the coordinator of the workshop.

"We are having trouble working with [Hagatha]," Cindy, the enrichment coordinator, told me on the phone.

"Oh no, what happened?" I asked with dread.

"I heard her complaining pretty loudly to some other volunteers. She asked 'How does someone get an interesting assignment around here? Do you have to be the queen of England?' I couldn't confront her at the time because there were patrons nearby. This one is going to be trouble."

Cindy could not have been more right.

We did not receive a request from Cindy that Hagatha be dismissed from the workshops, but she should have been. When Hagatha returned to my office after her third shift, she complained, "Some of the volunteers get treated so much better than the new people like me." She wanted me to take sides with her, but I stayed neutral. Henry, however, had a lot to say. He started barking as soon as he heard her voice.

"Henry, no. Simmer down," I pleaded. Hagatha's face was very serious, and she mostly ignored Henry this time. "Some of the volunteers have more experience, so they're given more complicated assignments," I tried to explain. "But I don't believe they are treated any differently. You are all important to us, whether you're brand new or seasoned. We need all you and value each of you."

"I don't think so. Come on, don't you agree that some of the volunteers think they are better than everyone else? I've also noticed that you have more time for them than you do for me," she complained.

"I'm sorry you feel that way. It's not true." Had I treated her badly? I hoped not, and genuinely tried to convince her, praying that Henry would not show any more disapproval. Although there was some bite in her tone, I sensed that she was hurt, and I wanted to fix her feelings.

Every Saturday, her mood was different. Some days she would come to me after her shift and report that she had been mistreated by the staff and volunteers. Some days she'd come to my desk in the morning before she started with gifts and sugary sweet compliments about how pretty I was and how cute and smart Henry was. She brought me a pearl necklace one morning that was still in the packaging from Overstock.com. She brought me a handmade quilt for Henry that looked and smelled like it had been used recently to line a cat litter box. The colors were pretty, and it was the perfect size for Henry. But I was afraid he'd catch some horrible disease from it, so I put it in a plastic bag and took it home to wash.

One morning as she was signing in at the computer, Hagatha was particularly chatty and told me about all the animals she had at home, which sounded like about twenty cats and ten dogs. Was she a collector, I wondered? Thanks to the recent popularity of reality TV shows like *Hoarders,* I knew a little about the bizarre behaviors of animal collectors.

From what I understood, hoarders were usually single people who lived alone with a lot of animals that didn't get proper nutrition or veterinary care. These people neglected not only the animals, but themselves as well. They often justified their behavior with the idea that the animals were surrogate children and that no one else would care for them. Hoarders often believed that if they did seek help, the animals would be euthanized. Based on what Hagatha had told me about her household, she fit the description.

Out of curiosity, I did a little research and found that pathological animal collecting was a form of mental illness. Hoarders can't deal with the thought of animals being euthanized and can't understand that what they are doing to the animals may be worse than death. They tend to be very secretive about how many animals they have and the condition of their home. This sounded familiar, because when we tried to get Hagatha's address and phone number for her file she would change the subject. When we insisted that we had to have a way to contact her in case of emergency, she gave three different addresses and phone numbers, and mumbled about which one she used the most.

When I first learned about this heartbreaking disorder, I took an inventory of my own living situation and examined my motives for having a house full of dogs. Fortunately, I didn't fit into all the psychiatric models that had been suggested for animal hoarding, which included the delusional model, suggesting that people who hoarded animals suffered from a highly focused form of delusional disorder, and the dementia model, which indicated warning signs for early stages of dementia. However, the addictions model, based on similarities to substance abuse, including a preoccupation with animals, denial of a problem, excuses for the behavior, and isolation bit at my heels. Being married to Don and having a very happy home life prevented me from slipping into a hazardous reality where the animals were concerned. Every one of my kids received excellent care from both Don and me. As long as I was in Don's care, I felt sure that I would not fall into the animal-collecting arena.

Hagatha's grimy clothes and wig, combined with her foul body odor, which reeked of animal feces, suggested that she suffered from this peculiar disorder. For fear of insulting her, I did not confront her about her personal hygiene. Since she was helping in the enrichment workshops, where the volunteers got pretty dirty building and painting devices that would be used by animals, I just let it go.

In the first year, we had a variety of problems with Hagatha, including her refusal to wear her name badge and proper uniform T-shirt, and her blatant negligence when she was reminded to submit her annual negative tuberculosis test. She also regularly "forgot" to sign in for shifts and resisted my efforts to teach her how to use the computer to do so. In addition to her lack of cooperation, we continued to get reports from staff and volunteers that she was very combative and hostile with patrons, staff and her fellow volunteers.

Practically everyone who dealt with Hagatha reported that she often complained about how badly the volunteer department treated her and was very negative about the zoo in general when in conversation with the patrons. Most of the people with whom she was once on friendly terms had stopped talking to her. One afternoon when she returned to our office to sign out after her orangutan watch shift, she defensively mentioned that staff and volunteers always gave her a hard time. She insisted that certain individuals were spies and that anything bad they might say about her were lies.

Her reports got harder to listen to when she insisted I favored the more experienced volunteers, and that we were ganging up on her. Then she accused me of "slighting" her for the concerns she brought to me, and for being "rude and cold." Comments like that went straight to my heart, because I am a people-pleaser. As a people-pleaser I tried so hard to make people happy that I lost the ability to keep healthy boundaries. As loony as she was, Hagatha had a keen sense of how to push my buttons. Her hostility escalated and I dreaded her Saturday visits. As she got more aggressive, Henry got more protective of me. When Hagatha entered the office and started cackling about her latest injustice, Henry's growls got louder and longer.

Her grumbling about my being "rude and cold" got nastier each week. Other people in the volunteer office could hear her, and I sensed that she wanted to pick a fight with me. As I was not a fighter, I did not respond, but her provoking insults and accusations of my being unpleasant and not caring about people drove me to the point where I had to protect myself by turning my back on her.

The volunteer sign-in computer sat on a table right in front of my desk and every week, Hagatha made a point of standing there longer than she needed to during her attempts to sign in and out.

"Can you help me sign in?" she whined. Initially I was glad to help her, as I was with all our volunteers, and I wanted to teach her the ropes, but after six months of her coming in every Saturday, I couldn't believe that she had not grasped the simple task of using the touch screen. She was bright enough to use the monitor easily, but she delighted in interrupting me, even if I was on the phone. My sense was that she wanted me to lose my cool so I'd lash out at her. Then she'd have something to hold against me.

As irritated as I got from Hagatha's unnecessary interruptions, I could not form words to express that her demands were getting ridiculous. Since she had started causing a scene every Saturday when she tried to sign in and out, I had stopped hushing Henry when he growled or barked. His vocalizations spoke for me.

"Okay, let's see what's going on here," I said as I approached the computer, making sure that the system was functioning properly. "It seems to be working. Do you want to go ahead and enter your ID number?" She did so and we made an assignment selection. "There you go. You're all set." My crisp body language did not hide that she was pushing me too far, but she just snickered.

"It wasn't working a minute ago," she defended herself with a smirk.

"Uh huh," I muttered and abruptly resumed my work. Her babbling continued, but I concentrated on my writing and didn't listen.

"Why are you ignoring me? You don't have time for us lowly new volunteers. If I were a more experienced volunteer you'd have more time for me, I bet."

Paralyzed by her mean spirit, I couldn't reply. All I could do was concentrate harder on the document on my computer screen. At this point Henry stood up from his little bed and leaned against my leg, which inspired me to take a deep breath and remember that I was fine. Henry's warm little body emitted a calming energy. My right hand automatically reached for his sweet little head, and I scratched behind his big ears.

"We're going to be fine," I whispered to him, hoping I would believe myself.

Some Saturdays, Henry and I would sneak out when we saw Hagatha coming down the hall and take a walk until she left the building. On those days, I usually found crumpled pieces of paper on my desk with her requests for my help written in pencil, usually in unintelligible, scratchy handwriting. The notes would say "Sign me—Sat 2 hours," or "Orang watch SAT." They never provided enough information for me to decipher what she wanted me to do. In fact, she never even wrote her name on them. I'd do my best to add her to the coming schedule, just to get her off my back, but she'd show up the following week and scold me for not helping her. Most of her requests were actions that could easily be taken care of with the touchscreen computer, but she would not learn how to use it. When I tried to call her at home to confirm her requests, the number would be out of service. She had neither cell phone nor email, which made it challenging to reach her. I resorted to good old-fashioned letters in the mail, but they would get sent back too with a stamp saying "Addressee unknown."

Unwilling to learn our computer-scheduling system, she would just show up for different assignments, even when she was not needed.

On a morning when she miraculously attempted to sign herself in, she stopped abruptly and asked "Why aren't there any assignments available to me? Do you hate me that much?"

"No, no, [Hagatha], we don't hate you. Please don't say that," I pleaded.

"Well, why is there nothing left for me to do?"

"Everything is just filled, that's all." The truth was that three coordinators from different departments had contacted me to make sure that Hagatha never returned to their department because she was a troublemaker. I had removed the sign-in options from the computer program on her account so she couldn't select assignments where she had been banned.

"I can't believe you refuse perfectly good volunteers. How can you do that? Don't you need us? How can you reject people who are offering to help for free?"

"I'm sorry . . . " Again, I didn't have words for her.

"I hope you have a nice day!" she croaked, heavy with sarcasm.

"You too, [Hagatha]," I replied. "Thank you for coming in today."

***

When Erin heard about all the trouble Hagatha was causing, she looked at her records and saw that Hagatha was six months overdue on her annual TB test. With this as fuel, she sent Hagatha a letter stating that she would be dismissed if she didn't comply with the city ordinance that required annual TB tests. Erin's efforts to protect me were comforting, and I appreciated that she stood up for me, but I feared that the letter would be returned to us as undeliverable, as all the mail sent to her had been. Two weeks later, when an outraged Hagatha rushed to my desk with the letter in her hand, I jumped.

"How dare you threaten to dismiss me? I'm a volunteer, you can't fire me!" Her ferocity was threatening, and panic bubbled up inside me. I tried to remind myself that Erin recently assured me that we had every right to insist on her TB test, as well as dismiss her, especially if she caused any more trouble.

My inability to please this woman robbed me of my dignity. *Why can't I make Hagatha happy? What's wrong with me?* Taking care of myself when I felt ineffective was impossible, so my physical strength faltered right along with my intellectual and emotional health. Henry tried to snuggle up to me when he sensed that I was distressed, but I was shutting down and didn't accept his efforts to help.

When Erin suggested that it was time to dismiss Hagatha for good, I was relieved. But her appearances at the zoo had become haphazard recently, so pinning her down to schedule a meeting to discuss it might be impossible. Therefore, Erin decided to write an official termination letter, stating our solid reasons for letting her go, and sent it certified to guarantee she got it.

Although Erin was younger than me by a decade, she felt like a big sister when she stood up for me and protected me from crackpots like Hagatha. Erin was more than just a good boss. Our work relationship was mutually respectful, but we also had a fun, healthy friendship. Her consistent "glass half-full" outlook on life kept me hopeful, much as Don's buoyant personality did.

Erin's support of my efforts to be free from Hagatha's nasty web showed me that the she had faith in my competence as a coordinator. Hagatha's bad behavior motivated Erin to take charge and assert her power in order to make things right, not just for me, but for all the departments that she impacted.

Hopefully, dismissing Hagatha would remove the black cloud that had been hovering over our department for months. With great relief, I deactivated her volunteer ID number in our system so she could no longer sign in. We sent the letter through the postal system with a "return receipt," to make sure she received it, and then we waited.

Three weeks passed and the letter didn't come back, which seemed like good news to me, but the next Saturday she appeared. Erin was not in, and I felt unsafe in Hagatha's presence. If she was angry, would she be violent? She approached the computer monitor and attempted to sign in without my help.

"My number isn't working." My heart sank, because this meant she had not received our letter. "Are you firing me?" she asked with trepidation. I had to confront her.

"Did you receive our letter a couple of weeks ago?" I asked, hoping to sound authoritative.

"What letter?" she asked, her voice shaking.

Please don't cry, Hagatha. I am already filled with guilt for letting you go, even though we should have done so months ago.

"We sent you this letter." I handed her a copy I had conveniently kept nearby in the event of this scenario. Hagatha grabbed the letter from my hand with so much hostility that Henry let out a growl from under my desk. Pretending that everything was normal, I sat back down and feigned interest in my computer screen. She opened the envelope and read the letter while standing in front of me. Tears ran down her face, then she started to dispute the points.

"None of these things are true," she said, holding the letter out to me.

"The best thing for you to do is make an appointment with Erin so you can discuss the specifics of your letter," I suggested. My hands were trembling, but I didn't think she could see them. Henry got closer to my leg then put his paws up on my knees, indicating that he wanted to get in my lap. His idea was a good one under the circumstances, so I rolled back in my chair, reached my arms out and said, "Lap Up, Henry." He did as he was told. "Good boy, Henry."

"There's your stupid little dog. What does *he* want?" she asked.

"He's just doing his job," I replied, feeling a little more protected.

"The comments from the keepers about my behavior are lies, and you know it."

As usual, she wanted me to fight with her, but all I could do was repeat my previous statement. "It really would be best if you call Erin to make an appointment to talk about this. I will email her right now to let her know you'll be calling. I'm sorry I can't schedule it for you, but I don't know her availability."

"You're heartless! You don't care about anyone!" she screeched.

I kept my composure, held Henry a little closer and refrained from arguing with her. His little warm body kept me grounded, but I was afraid of what Hagatha might do next.

"You've always been so rude and cold to me, and treated me badly. Where am I going to go?" Now she was crying and waving her arms around hysterically.

I felt like I'd been stabbed in the gut. No one had ever said anything like that to me. *Is she right? Am I heartless? Is she going to hit me?*

"I'm very sorry you feel that way," I said blankly, trying to hold myself together. My deadpan, emotionless responses pissed her off even more, but I was determined to keep my cool and not say anything she could hold against me.

"I'll see you soon," she threatened as she started to walk out. Even though she was quite angry, I was surprised at how shocked and hurt she was by our rejection. She looked desperate, as though she was going to die if she couldn't volunteer at the zoo. This pulled at my heart, but the insults that came from her mouth extinguished my compassion.

"Remember to wear your horns and your pointed tail. And don't forget your broomstick," she crowed. My trembling was now visible. Then she added, "You'll feel bad when I get killed in a car accident on the way home." And with that, she was gone.

Did she just imply that I was a devil *and* a witch? *Am I? What if she tries to hurt herself? Will it be my fault?* My heart felt as though it was pounding out of my chest, and I was sure I was going to pass out. I pulled Henry closer and started to cry. His presence calmed me in that moment, but I knew we were not finished with the Hagatha saga.

"Henry, why does she beat me up emotionally?" He listened attentively. "She is clearly a miserable person. All I can do is pray for her happiness and to let go of my fear of her, right?" As much as I dreaded a prospective, formal meeting with her and Erin, I knew that it would resolve this quagmire and life could get back to normal afterward. Never before had I felt so mistreated by someone I was supposed to be helping. My confidence plummeted further.

Erin was off, but she said I should call her at home if I had more trouble with Hagatha. When I called to tell her what had just happened, she was supportive and very protective of me, as always. We agreed that if Hagatha actually called to schedule a meeting to discuss the letter, we would both be in the room. Being confined in a small office with this mentally unstable woman scared me, but Erin assured me that we both needed to be there, if for no other reason than to act as witnesses. Who knew what this hostile woman was capable of?

***

Much to my amazement, Hagatha called Erin as soon as she got home that afternoon and left a message that she wanted to schedule a meeting. When Erin returned her call, they agreed to meet that Friday at 11:00 a.m.

"Should I bring Henry into the meeting?" I asked Erin on the big day, concerned that his presence would distract from our purpose.

"Hell yes!" she said.

"Thanks, I may need him if I pass out from fear," I said, only half joking.

Hagatha arrived ten minutes early for our meeting, and I felt my whole body tense up the second she walked in the door. Henry let out a little growl from underneath my desk. Hagatha looked alarmed and puzzled, unsure if she'd actually heard him, then gave me a cold stare.

"We might as well get started," Erin said when she saw that Hagatha had arrived. We all stepped into Erin's office, and she sat at her desk. Henry and I sat to the left of her desk and Hagatha sat on a chair facing us both. The meeting would give Hagatha an opportunity to defend herself and address the issues in the letter. With a pinched, bitter expression on her face, she started talking. She blamed the keepers and coordinators in all the different departments for making the volunteer assignments unpleasant.

"They wouldn't give me the good jobs. They saved those for the more experienced volunteers and practically ignored me. I had to keep changing assignments because I wasn't given enough to do. It was obvious that they just didn't like me." She was full of defensive words, which she had apparently given a lot of thought.

"I'm sorry that happened," Erin replied.

"If you heard that I was mean to patrons, it was a lie. I have always spoken respectfully to everyone at the zoo, even when *they* are rude to me like *this one*." She gestured to me. "You just want to get rid of me. You've always hated me."

Again she was stabbing me in the heart, but I remained blank. I kept eye contact with her as she talked for the next twenty minutes, contesting every point in the letter. She stumbled on her words and dropped the letter twice, which made me feel sorry for her, but I quickly remembered that she had the power to crush me.

"What is this part about me not wearing my proper uniform?" she asked pointing to the letter in her hand. "Maybe one time that happened when I needed to do laundry. I always wear the right shirt. This is a lie. You never talked to me about that. You could have at least given me a warning," she cackled.

"We went over uniform protocol in your training and on two separate occasions since then. How many conversations do you deem necessary for this?" Erin asked.

"This part that says I have been giving the wrong information to people about the animals is not true. I repeat what I hear other volunteers telling people. Nobody ever offered to teach me. Isn't that your job? You're not doing your jobs!"

Erin once again addressed Hagatha's inconsistencies with the sign-up procedures and her failure to show up for assignments. She also reminded her that we had the touchscreen computers available to volunteers so they could add themselves to the schedule.

"Leaving little slips of paper on Martha's desk with schedule requests for her to add is not the most efficient method, as sometimes the shifts you request in your notes are no longer available. Too much time is wasted trying to get a hold of you to reschedule, since you don't have email and your phone number doesn't work. If you had used the scheduling tool we provide, you could have seen the available shifts immediately. Martha has stopped what she was doing to help you on numerous occasions, showing you how to navigate through the system."

Thank you for defending me, dear Erin. I've not had to utter a word.

"If Martha weren't so sick, she'd be able to do a better job and help me," Hagatha blurted out.

My pounding heart nearly stopped. *Am I a bad employee because I'm sick? Is this all my fault? Is she right?*

"I'm sorry to say that you have progressed through all available assignments, and we no longer have anything for you. We're done here," Erin stated firmly and curtly, indicating that Hagatha's last comment about my being sick had upset her.

"Won't you please consider keeping me? I promise I'll be good," she pleaded, with an abrupt change in tone. Now she sounded like a child begging for mercy and her eyes got runny with tears.

"We're done here," Erin said again, making it clear that the meeting was over and our decision had been made.

"I think you are going to reconsider and call me to come back." Her voice and hands trembled as she stood up to collect her things. The pathetic quality she exhibited just moments earlier shifted back to hostility, and I didn't trust that she would leave the office peacefully. My heart pounded so hard I was afraid I was going to have a heart attack or pass out. Hoping to stay grounded, I had had my hand on Henry's back the whole meeting, but now I pulled him closer. He licked my wrist and peered up at me.

Before leaving Erin's office, Hagatha gave me a look so loaded with spite I was sure she had put a hex on me. Even though I was still holding my breath, I felt relieved the instant she was gone. Erin and I looked at each other and smiled in mutual support. We'd done it: we'd fired Hagatha! She was gone.

"I forgot my glasses," Hagatha said, suddenly appearing in the doorway. My heart stopped for second, then Henry let out a protective growl.

"Oh, that stupid dog. He shouldn't be allowed in here." She found her sunglasses on the floor near where she had been sitting, grabbed them and walked out.

"Is she gone?" I asked. Erin nodded. Henry growled.

"Good boy."

Hagatha made a few more attempts in the following months to return as a volunteer. On one occasion she delivered a messy, handwritten letter to the president of the zoo in which she accused me of treating her badly. Going over our heads didn't work for her, though, because the president trusted the decisions Erin and I made. When she showed up at the president's office with the slapdash letter, the president's assistant did her best to listen to Hagatha's complaint, but had a hard time taking her seriously because her crazy tilted wig was pulled up into cock-eyed pigtails, which made her appear nuts, to say the least.

Even though Hagatha had been dismissed as a volunteer, she was still able to come to the zoo as a visitor, which made me uneasy because I knew she might come to the office to terrorize me. Having Henry by my side was a huge comfort during the first few months after her banishment. Even though he was not supposed to growl at people, I had no intention of stopping him if she caused any trouble.

CHAPTER 16

Persecuted Fireplug

I WISH I COULD SAY that once Hagatha was gone, we never had any more difficult volunteers, but that would be a lie. Volunteering with animals attracts a rainbow of weirdos. Anyone who has ever been to a dog show or cat convention knows how odd animal lovers can be. We had our share of crazy cat ladies, dog whisperers, animal collectors, mad scientists, and retired schoolteachers.

Patrick was none of these. He was a middle-aged former Marine, who was built like a fireplug. When he first started the zoo's twenty-one-week volunteer training class, he was wide-eyed and willing, like his classmates, but after two weeks he started getting very vocal in class. He made references to his experience as a Marine and his homosexuality, as if he needed to defend himself. No one was challenging him, and as far as I knew none of his classmates or instructors had any issues with his sexual orientation. I wondered why he felt it was necessary to defend himself. I believed we needed more diversity in our ranks, so whenever he came into the office after class, I did my best to make him feel welcome.

Besides his puzzling defensiveness, Patrick liked to mention his gun collection a little too frequently, which was troubling.

Again, I wasn't sure why. Since he would not be my responsibility until he graduated from the class, I didn't put any notes in his file about these obvious red flags.

Patrick completed the class without any major incidents, but once he started touring school kids around the zoo, he got bristly, especially when he was with his mentor, Lew, a well-seasoned volunteer. He didn't like getting advice from Lew and felt Lew was too harsh with him about his touring style. Lew tried to let Patrick know that his animal facts were not always accurate and that he was taking too many liberties, embellishing the information he was supposed to teach.

Before long, Patrick complained to our head volunteer, Jean, a fair-minded woman who had been volunteering at the zoo for more than twenty years. As head volunteer, Jean was the direct supervisor for volunteers after they finished the class. Patrick complained to Jean that he was being scrutinized by Lew, and he was sure that it was because he was gay. What? Neither Jean nor I could believe our ears. Any criticism he had received was to help him on his tours and had nothing to do with his sexual orientation. Lew had been a volunteer for more than a decade, and although he was not particularly warm and fuzzy, he had never expressed any prejudice against gay people.

Patrick got very argumentative with Lew during their mentoring sessions. His anger bled into his tours, and he was abrupt and rude to patrons for no apparent reason. His hostility escalated so quickly that Jean determined that his presence on grounds with guests could be a liability. He was using foul language and insulting guests and staff.

So, like Hagatha, he received a written warning from Erin and Jean about his behavior. After three months, we were still hearing complaints from staff, guests and fellow volunteers about his hostility, so he received a second letter. Fortunately, he did not have any issues with me or Henry, so I was not the recipient of his anger, but if he was in the volunteer office, both Henry and I were on high alert. Although Henry did not growl when Patrick stormed in, he always rushed to my knees from his little bed and asked to Lap Up. I responded to Henry's requests with joy, and reinforced his behavior with a biscuit and a "Good boy!"

Patrick's behavior continued to cause problems. One Thursday, when his group gathered for their morning meeting before going out to tour, he announced to everyone that the zoo was intolerant of gay people. No one knew how to respond to him because they didn't know what he was talking about. When he got back from his tour, Jean invited him into her office to hear him out one more time. She listened patiently as he spewed his reports of being treated unfairly, then did her best to reassure him, but nothing she said convinced him that he was welcome at the zoo. He came out of their meeting thoroughly convinced that the entire zoo was against him because he was gay. His inability to be reasonable was bizarre. After he left for the day, Jean and Erin had a powwow and decided to dismiss him. His behavior was not changing. He continued to upset guests and the zoo couldn't afford bad press.

The next week Jean sat him down in her office, explained everything very calmly, then gave him his letter of dismissal. He grabbed the letter out of her hand and said, "There will be consequences, I assure you. You can't get away with dismissing me. I know this is because I'm gay. My attorney will be in touch with you." And with that he stomped out. Henry stood up, let out a little growl and came to Lap Up.

The next day Patrick came back in looking for Jean, but she was not in, so I tried to help him. He wanted to discuss his situation. His face was red and his expression twisted. Was he carrying a gun or some other weapon? He reminded me that he was being discriminated against and that we would be hearing from his attorney. I was not afraid of his attorney, but I was terrified of his anger. *Please don't yell at me, Patrick. Please don't tell me I'm incompetent or that I don't care.* My hands started shaking and I reached down to touch Henry for comfort. Just feeling his warm little body slowed my breathing temporarily.

After Patrick spat out his angry words, he realized that I was not the decision maker and stomped out. Thankfully, he left without pulling out any weapons. As I held my hand on Henry's back he squirmed around to face me, then put his paws on my knees to Lap Up. By this time my shaking was accompanied by a pounding heart and an overwhelming faintness. My head went down to my desk and Henry jumped from my lap to the floor and started barking and howling like an alarm. He was performing one of his learned tasks, "summon a coworker," which until this point he had never had to do. Twenty seconds later, Mary, one of the education department staff members from the next office, came running in. She was aware of this task because I had informed everyone who worked in the immediate area that if Henry let out a howling bark, they should come see if I needed help.

Once Mary arrived Henry returned to putting his little paws on my knees to get back to my lap. Mary came to my side and asked if I was okay.

"Yeah, I got scared by Patrick, the volunteer we just fired. He came in to intimidate me, and it worked. I was afraid I was going to pass out, but I think I'm okay. Thanks, Mary."

"Can I get you some water? Do you need me to dial 911?" she asked.

"No, but thank you. I'm going to be okay. At least I'm breathing more normally now. I came close to passing out, but I'm okay. Thank you." At this point I turned to Henry and reassured him with a hug. "Thank you, buddy, good job."

Patrick stayed away from the zoo for the next three months. Each day that passed that we didn't hear from him or Hagatha, I breathed a little easier. One afternoon, Jean opened the mail and came to my desk to show me a letter from Patrick. Without any mention of all the trouble he had caused, his letter stated that he was resigning because he no longer had time to volunteer. We had already deactivated him in our system because he had been terminated, so his letter was unexpected and odd. If our legal department ever received anything about a discrimination lawsuit from him, I was never told. I hoped and prayed that we had seen the last of the crackpots for a while.

CHAPTER 17

Promotions Panic

THE BIGGEST STRESSOR IN my job was dealing with the occasional screwballs like Hagatha and Patrick, but I was lucky because Erin always had my back. She knew what to do when difficult situations came my way, because she had done my job for years before becoming the manager. However, shortly after we resolved the Hagatha and Patrick issues, Erin and I found ourselves facing circumstances with which neither one of us had any experience.

The ground started to rumble when the zoo suffered some severe budget cuts. Right away, a big group of people were laid off and many others received warnings. Luckily neither Erin's nor my job was in jeopardy, but that didn't mean we would be spared from turmoil. The coming months would bring huge, departmental changes that would have significant impact on both of us.

To generate more revenue, the zoo's top brass hired an enterprising team of promotions people, who turned things upside down. They were experts in strategic branding and cutting-edge social-media marketing. At first, I was excited and supportive because their efforts would help the zoo grow, and I didn't think we would be affected. I was dead wrong.

This new team of innovative individuals swept in and started introducing their brilliant concepts, ruffling the feathers of many departments. Part of their plan was to create new on-site events that would spawn attention and get more people through the gates. Erin and I were accustomed to staffing about a dozen traditional events per year, but these new people, who were still learning how the zoo operated, seemed to think the volunteer department would supply endless free labor, and started making requests for unrealistic numbers of people to "work" their activities. While I tried to process all the changes and please this new team, my stress level went through the roof, as did my dependence on Henry.

One afternoon Erin, Henry, and I attended a promotions function to celebrate all the changes. Trying to keep an open mind and remain willing, something that Erin did so effortlessly, I trudged up to the main administration building to attend the shindig with Henry at my side. As we entered the crowded room Henry clung to my leg. He seemed so tiny is the sea of long, human legs. We tried to make our way to the refreshment table for a soda, but couldn't get through the crowd, so I just stopped and took a breath.

Staff members from every department were there, including the president, CFO and new VP of marketing, all whom scared the bejesus out of me. But as always, I held my head up high and pretended I was confident and comfortable. Before long the promotions people would make an announcement about the festivities they were planning. That was all well and good for them, but I knew that whatever they had in mind was going to put more demands on us, and I worried that I would not be able to deliver.

Sure enough, within five minutes, Kasey, the big cheese in charge of promotions, started to clink a fork on her glass so she could make her announcements. As soon as she started talking, my legs went weak. Her appearance and demeanor were soft and mom-like, not intimidating at all. She wore jeans and flowing blouses and had a casual style, but her energy and expertise in business promotion were ferocious and fearless.

"Hello everyone. Thank you for coming today," Kasey said in a calm, self-possessed manner. "We're really excited about the new projects on the horizon, and as you know, we're going to need everyone's support and cooperation as we move forward. Thank you for all you've done already and thank you in advance for helping with the cool events we have coming." She started applauding the staff to show her appreciation.

"Uh oh," I whispered to Erin, knowing we were about to get some daunting assignments. Erin kept a stiff upper lip. I envied her courage and fortitude.

"Our cool new holiday events are going to start in November and go through January, and for those activities we're going to need about fifty volunteers per night," Kasey said, giving me a wink.

Without thinking, I laughed out loud. *She's kidding, right?*

The smile was gone from her face.

She means it. She's dead serious. Fifty volunteers per night? How are we going to do that? Just keep smiling. Don't let anyone see how scared you are. Even though she spoke in a soft, easy manner, she exuded self-confidence. She maintained a very down-to-earth quality, and I genuinely liked her and wanted to please her, but at the same time, she terrified me.

In previous years Erin and I had provided twenty-five volunteers per shift for a total of *four days* for *two weekends,* not *fifty volunteers per night for seven weeks!* There was no way we could get the numbers that Kasey was requesting. I looked at Erin's face to see if I could detect any trace of shock, but she wore the same smile I did. *What is she thinking? Does she think we can do it?*

We had a healthy corps of dedicated volunteers, and the promotions department assumed they were always available and would all happily sign up for additional events. What they didn't know was that most of our volunteers had existing, ongoing assignments and no interest in helping with special events. People came to volunteer at the zoo because they loved animals. The new events had nothing to do with animals. Their purpose was to generate crowds, like spectacles at an amusement park. Volunteers were needed for crowd control and to give directions. Neither of these assignments appealed to volunteers who were there to do research or educate people about conservation and species preservation.

A month earlier, I had worked hard to recruit volunteers for the first of these new events. Even though asking them to help seemed insensitive, I did it anyway. When they said no, I respectfully accepted their responses and knew not to push them. When a few generous individuals agreed to help out, I was overjoyed and grateful, but when I learned from some of them afterward that they had been treated badly by "the people in charge," I cringed. They told me they had been scolded like children for chatting with their fellow volunteers while at their crowd-control posts. One said he'd been reprimanded and humiliated for straying from his post for a few minutes. I didn't push to find out who they meant by "the people in charge," but I worried it was the new promotions people. My fear was that the new staff members didn't know how to speak to the volunteers. This pained my soul because I had spent years nurturing healthy, respectful relationships with each of my volunteers so they would feel valued and appreciated.

Managing volunteers was very different from managing paid employees. When speaking to them, I always kept in mind that their compensation for helping with any assignment was the joy they felt while doing it. So it was up to me to make sure they were doing something they enjoyed. In addition to that, I made sure to acknowledge their efforts genuinely and frequently. When I needed them to do something, I always asked as if it was a huge favor, and I meant it. Acknowledging a person's efforts and enthusiasm was crucial. Unless they were breaking some rule or endangering themselves, a visitor, or an animal, I tried my hardest to never reprimand or discipline them. The teenagers were a different story, of course. They didn't want to be there in the first place. Most of them were just earning volunteer hours for their college applications, and by nature, they were a little unruly. Fortunately, they were not my responsibility.

Kasey started announcing more upcoming events and all the changes we could expect to see in the next six months. Again I looked at Erin, hoping she would be as stunned as I was, but she just kept smiling. *Does Erin think I can handle this? If my volunteers sign up for more of these new events and "the people in charge" bark orders at them, the news is going to spread like wildfire through the ranks and nobody will want to help out. This is all going to fall on my shoulders and crush me.*

Maybe my fear is just getting the better of me. There have only been a few isolated incidents. Calm down. Does this all seem impossible because I'm run down, or are these demands unreasonable?

My chest tightened and I felt dizzy and disoriented. My heart was telling me to leave the room before I passed out, but I couldn't remember where the exit was. Right at that moment, Henry stood on his hind legs, put his front paws on my knees and looked me in the eyes. He sensed my distress so I gave him the command, "Let's get out of here," my slang version of his task "Find the Exit." He started pulling me to the nearest open door. Once he started tugging me, I got my bearings and knew which way to go. Without saying goodbye to Erin or any of my colleagues, Henry and I walked back to our office.

My panic during the party was not a surprise, but until it happened I thought I'd be okay. Back at my desk I calmed down a little because I was no longer surrounded by people, but I was still anxious about the future and all I could see was black, so I gave Henry another command to Lap Up.

In a heartbeat, he was in my lap, aggressively licking my face. The tactile stimulation provided a Reality Affirmation for me, another of Henry's tasks.

I texted Erin that I was going home sick, but before I left my desk, Henry performed one more task, which he did daily without a command from me. With his nose, he nudged my lunch bag toward me, reminding me to eat. He knew to nudge it because it had not been moved from where I put it when we arrived that morning. If I was to move it at any point during the day, it would indicate to him that I had eaten, but since it was in the same place, he put his snout behind it and pushed it toward me. I was forgetting to feed myself more frequently since the changes had started, especially when I got overwrought. My frantic daily dashes to the bathroom had increased as well, which ruined my appetite. So, in response to Henry's prod, I sat down to eat my half peanut butter sandwich.

Once I was done, I packed up my things so we could leave, but my body and mind were numb. How much longer would I be able to pretend I had the strength to do my job? Why was everything so hard?

We walked to my car, and after I put Henry in his crate, I got in the driver's seat and burst into tears. "I don't like what's happening, buddy. I'm not sure I like my job anymore," I confided to Henry. Falling out of love with my job was so disheartening I didn't want to think about it.

"Should we drive over to the campus and go for a walk?" He wagged his tail, willing and eager. Several months earlier, I had discovered a beautiful college campus, which was useful when I needed somewhere to go to de-stress after work. Even though Henry helped me get through the rough periods throughout the day, I found that when I left work, I needed to decompress.

When we had first explored the grounds, I was stunned to find this haven of tranquility just two miles from home. The stately old buildings and big trees transported me back to carefree days of early childhood, when we lived in a college town. The wide sidewalks winding through the green lawns welcomed me, even though I was not a student. Lying down on the grass and doing yoga with Henry often calmed me down, so I tried to get there every day.

Luckily the campus was only a ten-minute drive from work. After parking, I put Henry's leash on, then he looked up at me with his big, brown chihuahua eyes, and waited for his next command.

"Heel, buddy."

He went straight to my left side and paid close attention because he knew I was still on shaky ground. Hearing tension in my voice prompted him to push his little twelve-pound body as close to my leg as possible.

The dialogue in my head started up immediately as we entered the well-groomed campus and headed for our favorite patch of grass near the outdoor amphitheater. But something was different about one of the voices. As it responded to my fearful thoughts, it didn't berate me or fuel the fire. Instead, it offered insight.

Something has to change or you're going to have a heart attack.

What am I supposed to do? What can I change? Taking time off from work is not going to change things. I'm still going to be weak and terrified of failing. The pressure will still be there when I get back.

Henry and I reached our spot and we lay down on the nice, soft grass. The weather was perfect for yoga: calm and warm.

Why is everything so hard? I can barely do my job anymore, my body and mind are falling apart, and it's hard to drag my sorry self around.

You're going to get fired for sure, and you'll never be able to find another job. Who would hire an anxious, emaciated person like you?

I couldn't hold down a job anyway. The only reason I'm still at the zoo is because Erin is so understanding and accommodating. Nobody in their right mind would hire me now.

What are you so afraid of?

I don't know. Running out of money, being homeless, or being sent to prison for impersonating a normal, healthy person.

What's your absolute worst fear?

Being destitute or forgotten. Dying, I guess.

But isn't that what you want, essentially? To be dead?

Yeah.

So, if you experience your worst fear and die, you will be exactly where you want to be, right?

I guess so.

So why be so scared all the time? Death is the ultimate freedom from your misery here on Earth. Everything you are so scared of now will be completely meaningless once you're dead. In fact, if you can step back from your fear of failing at work and see how meaningless it all is, you would realize that you are already free. Can you do that just for a minute?

How?

Just stop giving your fear so much power. To heck with all the demands at work. Fuck that. So what if they fire you? Why don't you just quit? If all your fears manifested themselves, you would be free. So to heck with them.

You're right. I just can't do it anymore. To heck with it! Fuck it.

Good girl. You'll be okay. Don still has a job. You two live so frugally, you'll manage.

That's true.

Don would much rather have you stop working and be healthy than earning money and getting sicker. He'll support whatever you have to do to get better, right?

He will.

Think about it. In all your years on Earth, have you ever been homeless?

No.

Have you ever run out of money?

No.

The universe has always taken care of you, right? So why would it stop now? You have no worries, no cares. Just relax now with Henry here on the grass and try to believe that just for a minute. Can you do that?

Sure.

Your fears are just products of your exhaustion and you are letting your job kill you.

I suppose.

If you turn all your fears over to the universe and still end up miserable, alone, and homeless, then you have my permission to kill yourself.

That sounds fair.

As I lay in the grass with Henry, staring at the clouds passing overhead, a huge weight lifted off me when I realized that I could kill myself. Paradoxically, knowing that ending my life was an option liberated me. For a brief moment, I could see that my work-related fears were insignificant and not worth the energy I gave them.

My euphoric freedom only lasted a few minutes that afternoon, but it flashed back into my mind periodically for the next few days. I tried to revisit the thoughts that precipitated the onset of that feeling whenever I could. And even though I couldn't conjure up that feeling on demand, at least I could remember that I had *once* felt it. I knew that I was capable, even for a brief period, of letting go of my fears, of entirely trusting that I'd be okay. The manifestation of my worst fears could bring me to ultimate freedom. From then on, my walks with Henry on the campus became a mission to revisit the peace I found that day.

CHAPTER 18

Cassie

WHEN ALL THE EXCITEMENT about new events at the zoo started, I could maintain a calm front because I thought the changes would be temporary. If I could weather the storm, I was sure that things would die down. But after a year of jumping through hoops to keep up with the requests for volunteers, my façade started to crumble. As the work pressure increased, my weight dropped, and I was experiencing more anxiety, which triggered faintness, so my doctors urged me to take a long leave of absence to recuperate. I didn't disagree with their sentiment, but I wasn't ready to give up quite yet.

Then something happened that sparked my enthusiasm to stay engaged in life. One of my absolute favorite people at the zoo was a feisty little woman named Libby. Educated at Harvard and born with a razor-sharp wit, she was not only an awesome writer and editor, she was also a dynamic conversationalist. Whenever I found myself talking with Libby, which was usually about some fascinating bug she had recently encountered or some unique. succulent plant she was adding to her garden, I felt smart. Even if I didn't fully understand everything she said, I was flattered that she thought I might. Her knowledge of plants and insects was amazing. I didn't share most of it, but when she talked about her cats or any of the animals at the zoo, I jumped right in.

Libby once likened herself to the lowland anoa, a small water buffalo found in Indonesia, because they were "solitary animals that, if cornered or approached within a critical distance, would turn and attack violently." I had never seen this side of her.

On a Wednesday afternoon in July, as I was struggling to wrangle all my assignments at work without having an anxiety attack, I got an email from Libby. My name was one of a dozen names on the list of recipients, all whom were zoo employees, and it was sent from Libby's personal email address, which meant it had personal significance. The email was a cry for help. One of our animal keepers, Karen, a kindhearted, hardworking lover of animals, had been recently diagnosed with a terminal brain tumor. The doctors estimated that she only had six weeks to live. This news was especially shocking because she was just a couple years older than me. A few months earlier, she had taken an early retirement and was in the prime of her life. How could someone so young and vibrant be so close to death? Hearing about her imminent demise gave me a brief appreciation for my own life.

Libby's email was a plea to find friends who could help foster Karen's pets. She had two cats, three dogs, two horses and a king vulture, all whom needed immediate care and eventually new homes. Karen had deteriorated so quickly that she was already in hospice care. What kind of dogs, I wondered? There was no way I could bring cats into our house, nor could we stable a horse, and since I knew nothing about vultures, I couldn't offer to take him, but I could help with one of the dogs. As I read further into the email I learned that there was an elderly Pug named Olive, a five-year-old terrier mix named Syd, and a large six-year-old female German shepherd-lab mix named Cassie. Having a second big dog to keep Dixie company when Don, Henry, and I left for work every day sounded like a great idea, so I immediately responded to Libby's email to tell her I wanted to help.

Right after I hit "send," a pang of guilt rushed through me. I should have asked Don how he would feel about all this. He might not like the idea. He might not want another dog. So I emailed him explaining Karen's tragic circumstances, hoping it would have the same impact on him that it had on me. Don and

I had only two dogs at the time, since we lost dear Arty to old age a year earlier, and for so much of our time together we had been a three-dog family. The universe was sending Cassie to be the third. Hopefully Don would see it that way too.

Within five minutes Don responded to my email, and I was relieved to see he shared my sentiment! I was all set to get Cassie and bring her home when I realized that I had not even met her yet. What if she was mean or sick? What if she didn't get along with Dixie or Henry? Taking a minute to breathe, I emailed Libby again and asked, "Okay, what's next? When can I meet Cassie?" Two minutes after I sent my email my cell phone rang.

"I'm going to Karen's house tonight after work to feed all the animals. Do you want to come?" Libby asked.

"Yes, absolutely. Where does she live?"

"In Burbank, not far from the equestrian center. Thank you so much for helping. Cassie is a great dog." She gave me the address, and we agreed to meet at 5:30 at Karen's house.

The area of Burbank near the equestrian center was one of my favorite places, and I often took Henry there for walks after work. The streets were lined with big trees and there wasn't much traffic. The houses were well cared for, but not large or ostentatious, and I was surprised and delighted to learn that many of them had stables in their back yards. Henry and I often saw people riding or walking their horses down the street, which somehow gave me a peaceful feeling. On occasion, I would see someone walking what looked like a big dog, but when I got closer I would see it was actually a miniature pony. How could I not smile when I saw these cute little horses trotting down the street? Sometimes I saw people in little carts or buggies being pulled by ponies.

Henry and I found Karen's house and looked for Libby's white Honda Civic. Since I didn't see it yet, we waited in the car and looked around. The houses on Karen's street were small and close together. It surprised me that there was a stable in the back of her little house. When Libby's car pulled up, I told Henry to stay put for a minute so I could meet Cassie without him. Henry was a good sport. I was about to walk into a house full of animals I'd never met, and I didn't want to subject him to a potentially chaotic environment.

"Hi, thanks for coming," Libby said, "we've been overwhelmed by all this since Karen got sick." The "we" she was referring to was herself and two of Karen's animal keeper friends from the zoo, Robert and Wanda, who had stepped up to the plate three days earlier when Karen was rushed to the hospital after losing consciousness. Since Karen was single and had no children, there was no one to take care of all her animals.

"Does she have family?" I asked.

"Her mom is around, but they don't get along," Libby explained. At that point, I knew it was better to not ask any more nosy questions, but Libby shared, "Karen is closer to her friends than she is to her family."

"I'm so sorry this is happening. I don't really know Karen very well, but I'd like to help. It's so nice of you guys to do all this."

"The doctors don't expect her to live more than six weeks, so Robert, Wanda, and I have to clean out her house and find homes for all the animals," Libby explained.

"You're good friends," I said. "I can't wait to meet Cassie."

"Come on in," Libby said as she unlocked Karen's front door. We were greeted by Syd, the five-year-old brown terrier mix, who looked like he could be in a production of "Annie." He was friendly and welcoming. Right behind him was a wiggling, round pug.

"This is Olive. She's really old and blind," Libby said referring to the pug, "but she gets around pretty well."

"Where's Cassie?" I asked.

"She's probably hiding in the laundry room out back," Libby explained, leading me through Karen's messy kitchen to the dark, cluttered living room and out to the back yard, where two horses stood behind a wooden fence. Karen had only been gone for three days, but there was a thick layer of dust covering everything, which made it look like no one had been there for months. The whole house had a forgotten, dreary feeling. I would later learn that Karen had been suffering from a terrible depression prior to getting her brain tumor. My compassion grew, knowing that Karen and I had depression in common, and that made me even more eager to adopt Cassie.

"Cassie . . . " Libby called into a little room off the back yard. "Here she is."

Crouching down next to the washing machine was an eighty-five-pound, golden dog who looked very scared.

"Hi, honey." I approached her gently with my hand out for her to sniff. "How are you?" Cassie's sad brown eyes looked up at me, then she stood and came toward me to have a sniff. Her size overwhelmed me as I sat on the floor next to her, but she was gentle.

"All the dogs are freaked out because they can't find Karen," Libby explained. It looked as though Cassie was taking it the hardest. Her face looked so sad, but she accepted my invitation to be petted, and she let me scratch her ears.

"Aww, what a good girl. Hey, honey, can we be friends? Do you want to come home with me? Oh, Libby, I love her already. When can I take her home to meet Don and our other pets?"

"We'll figure that out. I'll need to talk to Robert and Wanda," Libby replied.

"I hope soon. Tomorrow after work I could come get her for a trial run. Can I take her on a walk right now?" I asked, eagerly, hoping she would be willing. I also needed to know I could manage her. "Does she have a leash?"

"Probably somewhere in this mess. Let me look." Libby went looking for a leash, and I continued to rub Cassie's ears. She was starting to trust me already and leaned her full weight into my legs, almost knocking me over. I had never had a dog as large as Cassie. Gus, the largest, had been fifty-five pounds at his chubbiest. Would I be able to handle her? Was she going to pull me off my feet?

"Here you go." Libby said, handing me an old leash coated in cobwebs. "I'm not sure if Karen took these guys on walks. I think she took them to the dog park."

"Come here, Cassie! Want to go for a walk?" The leash interested her, but she still looked tentative. Syd came bouncing over to me, letting me know he wanted to go too. "Sorry, Syd, I can't handle two of you at the same time." I hooked the leash onto Cassie's thick, red collar and led her to the front door. She walked out willingly as Libby held Syd inside, and we ventured out to the sidewalk. When she saw the small patch of grass in front of the neighbor's house, she dove onto her side and rolled around in ecstasy. I was happy to see her so joyful. But to find out if I could handle her on the leash, I had to persuade her to finish rolling around and start walking.

We got to the corner, two houses down, without Cassie pulling me off my feet, but her next move puzzled me. All of a sudden she perked up her ears, looked around, and then, with great determination, she decided she needed to go back home. My hope was that a nice walk would get her mind off missing Karen, but for some reason right at the corner she turned around and pulled me back to the house. Not wanting to traumatize her, I followed her lead, and we went back.

This seemed like a good time for Henry to meet her. He was waiting patiently in his crate in the car. After putting Cassie back inside the house, I got Henry.

"Come on Henry; let's go meet your new sister."

When we walked through the door, Syd, Cassie, and a stumbling Olive approached Henry. No one growled, but there was cautious sniffing all around. Within sixty seconds, they all wanted to play, and I knew there wouldn't be any fighting. Cassie was a gentle giant, not aggressive by any means.

"Tomorrow I can come and walk her again, if you want me to."

"That would be great," Libby said. "Thank you so much. As you can see we really have our hands full here. What a mess. The animals need so much attention and care. We also have to go through all Karen's things and sort everything out since she won't ever be coming home."

"That's huge. I'm so sorry. Please let me know if there is anything else I can do to help."

"Karen kept everything. You can see by all the junk and dust all over the place. I think it's safe to say she was a hoarder."

"Yeah, I guess so," I agreed. "Okay, I better get home now to feed my menagerie, but I'll be back tomorrow to walk this big girl. Bye, my sweetie." I wrapped my arms around Cassie's huge neck and gave her a kiss on the head. "Bye, Libby, you are a good friend to help Karen so much."

"Thanks again, see you tomorrow."

As I drove home my heart was filled with excitement and love. "Henry, you are going to have a new sister." At that moment, I knew that to take care of Cassie and help Libby and Karen, I would have to make an effort to eat more and keep my strength up. With that in mind I opened a bottle of chocolate Ensure and took a big sip. Why not get started right now?

Every day after work, I went to walk Cassie. Teaching her some obedience was imperative if I wanted to feel confident walking her, because she was so strong. As soon as I put her leash on, she'd get excited and pull me out the front door. By the end of the first week, she trusted me enough to let me take her around the block. She had quickly learned how to heel and sit, so I stopped worrying about being yanked off my feet. I was already totally in love with her, so I asked Libby again when I could take her home.

"Robert and Wanda want all the animals to stay at the house until Karen passes away." This disappointed me, but what could I say? Until it was time to take Cassie home, I visited and walked her every day after work. I hoped that my love and attention could help her cope with losing Karen.

During the five weeks I helped with Cassie, I had a strong sense of purpose and knew I had to take care of myself. Otherwise I would not be able to provide a safe new home for her. Being in Karen's home was eerie, because all her things were just where she left them on the day she was rushed to the hospital. She would never be back. But instead of letting myself get stuck in the sadness of the situation, I focused on Cassie and all the love and energy she had to give. She was still very much alive, and I was reminded that I was too.

While Karen was in hospice, her visitors were limited to immediate family and her closest friends, Libby, Robert, and Wanda. That was mostly a relief. As much as I wanted to assure Karen that Cassie and the other animals would be getting good homes, I knew I couldn't handle seeing someone who was rapidly dying. She wouldn't have known me anyway.

Seeing the sad faces of Libby, Robert, and Wanda every afternoon as they sifted through Karen's personal belongings, deciding what her estranged family might want to keep, was really grim. I knew that it was a hundred times harder for them.

When the time came for the animals to go to their new homes, I was both sad and happy. Karen died peacefully in her sleep, almost six weeks to the day of her terminal diagnosis. The two horses would be going to a ranch, the two cats found a home with one of Karen's animal keeper friends, Syd was going to be fostered by Erin, and the king vulture was going to an eccentric artist who had an emu and knew a lot about large birds. Sadly, Olive the pug had to be euthanized, because she would not have survived a move.

Bringing Cassie home was a joyous event. On a warm, sunny Sunday in early September, I met Libby, Robert, Wanda, and Erin at Karen's house. When I arrived, Cassie met me at the door, whimpering with excitement, ready to go for her daily walk. Her warm greeting made me proud of the progress we had both made in the past five weeks. She was no longer pining over Karen's absence, although I'm sure she still missed her, and I had been making efforts every day to feed myself.

Both Syd and Cassie would be going to their new homes on this day as well. Robert and Wanda thanked both Erin and me profusely for adopting Syd and Cassie. I wanted to thank them because Cassie's presence in my life was giving me a reason to live, but that sounded so dramatic that I kept it to myself.

Erin and her husband Sean had brought their dog Thor, a German shepherd, to meet Syd before they all went home together. After Syd and Thor amiably sniffed each other, we all went for a little walk around the block. I'd been looking forward to this day for weeks. Libby, Robert, and Wanda still had several more weeks of work to do in the house, which would be painfully sad. In the five weeks I'd watched them pack up Karen's belongings and find homes for her animals, I witnessed a level of true friendship I had never seen before. Cassie would always remind me of that.

Cassie coming into my life at a time when I was so exasperated was no accident. The poignancy of Karen's death cast some light on my need to make self-care my first priority, but it was just a flicker, and I still couldn't see what I needed to do.

CHAPTER 19

Time for Change

CASSIE GOT ALONG WELL with Henry and Dixie, and quickly became a member of our pack. I wasn't surprised, since she had been living peacefully with cats and dogs at Karen's, but if she had gotten aggressive with them, we would have had a problem. At eighty-five pounds, she had a huge advantage over Dixie, who was barely fifty pounds, and Henry, who was just eleven. But she only used her size when she wanted to show love. She did this by leaning into my legs, nearly knocking me over, and jumping onto the couch to get closer to me when I watched TV. She was such a good-natured dog, and her presence in our lives felt right from the minute she came home. However, I could tell she missed Karen, because she occasionally paced, as though she was looking for her. Don and I gave her a lot of hugs and attention, and after a few weeks, the pacing stopped and she looked less anxious.

As much as Cassie's presence lifted my spirits, the stress from work continued to wear me down. Every day I got more requests from the promotions department to staff their upcoming activities, and every day I struggled to stay on top of things. The harder I tried to keep up, the weaker I got. My thinking was muddled and I couldn't concentrate for more than a few minutes at a time. I knew I needed to make some changes, but didn't know where or how to start.

When I complained to my doctors, they just insisted that I take time off work, but my Midwestern work ethic stubbornly resisted. I couldn't yet grasp the idea that taking a medical leave didn't mean I was failing or giving up. I didn't understand that letting go of work would give me a chance to live again.

One evening, as I was trying to read an email from our promotions coordinator, I found that I couldn't make sense of it. I read the email three times, but the words looked like gibberish and I couldn't understand any of them. My chest tightened and my breathing got shallow, then I heard Erin locking her office door.

"You should have left hours ago," she said as she headed out. "Just turn off your computer and go home."

"I have a few more emails to send, and then I'll head out, I promise."

I was lying. I still had too much to do to get ready for Featured Creatures, one of the zoo's special events that started the next day. I had to make sure there would be enough volunteers to help with activities throughout the zoo.

There's no way you can get all the volunteers they've asked for. You're going to let them down, the mean voice in my head reminded me. *If you don't find enough volunteers, the event will be a failure and it will be all your fault. Everyone will know how truly incompetent you are and you'll be fired.*

For reasons I never understood, Erin had confidence in me. Maybe that was because she couldn't hear the undermining voices in my head. Erin told me on a regular basis that I was doing a good job, but I couldn't believe her because the voices were too loud. My fear of failing had taken over my thoughts, but Erin wasn't worried at all. She never worried about my work or her own. She always believed that things would be fine. I wished I had the strength and confidence that she thought I had.

Another email came in. It was from a volunteer canceling for the next day's event. This was bad, because we were already short of people for the morning shift. I would need to find someone to replace her, which meant staying even longer. My heart started pounding.

The phone rang. My chest tightened when I saw the caller ID. It was the promotions coordinator. What was she doing there so late?

"Volunteer department, this is Martha," I said cheerfully as I picked up the phone.

"Oh good, you're still there. I hate to do this to you, sweetie, but we need about five more volunteers for the morning shift tomorrow because we have a special group of patrons coming in," she explained.

"I'll do what I can, but I can't make any promises," I said, trying to sound calm as my hands started shaking. *Five more volunteers by 7:30 the next morning?*

"Good girl. I know you can do it. You're the best, Martha. How's Henry?" she asked.

"He's good, thanks." I reached down and patted his head. He was still curled up on his little dog bed under my desk. "Okay, let me get going on this. I'll see you tomorrow," I said before she could ask for anything else.

"Thanks again!" She hung up. *You can't let her down. You've never let her down.*

My rational mind told me that if I didn't succeed, it wouldn't be the end of the world. I wasn't an ER doctor. Nobody's life was depending on my success. No one would die if I couldn't find enough volunteers for the next day. No one would even be hurt. But I was terrified of disappointing anyone. I was terrified of disappointing myself. I wasn't sure which was worse.

Another email came in. This one was from a volunteer asking to switch to the afternoon shift for the event. Fearing that I could lose him altogether, I emailed right back and said, "That's fine, come when you can! Thanks so much for helping." My head started spinning and I couldn't catch my breath. I was down to seven people for the morning and I needed at least fifteen. *They're going to fire you for sure. You'll be jobless and homeless and end up living on the street, begging for money to buy dog food.* My eyes welled up with tears and I worried that I was going to faint.

"Lap Up, Henry." I called. "Lap Up." I patted my leg. Sweet little Henry jumped up on command and started licking my face. The sensation of his wet tongue on my nose, lips and cheeks brought me back to reality for the moment, and I took a deep breath. My head stopped spinning.

"Thanks, Henry," I held him close. "I'm okay." Relieved that I hadn't fainted, I sat back in my chair and let myself cry, loudly. Henry gave me one more lick and stared into my eyes. "I'm fine buddy, thanks. You're a good boy."

When I tried to focus on my computer screen, nothing made sense, which told me it was time to go home. "Let's get out of here, buddy. I can't think straight anymore." I glanced through my emails to make sure no one else had canceled, then closed out all the windows on my computer and powered down. After double-checking my voicemails, I made a few notes about the orientation I'd be giving to volunteers the next day. Before I left, I gathered my pens, stapler, and tape dispenser and locked them in a drawer. Once my desk was nice and tidy and everything was in its place, I could go.

Before I stood up Henry nudged my lunch bag toward me.

"You're right, guy. I forgot to eat. No wonder I can't concentrate."

Henry whined and let out a little "Ruff."

"Thanks Hank. I need to eat." But the problem was deeper than that. A momentary rise in my blood sugar would not restore my strength or my ability to concentrate. Henry was doing his best to remind me, but it was up to me to stop pushing myself so hard.

"I promise I'll eat my sandwich when we get home, Henry. Right now, I just need to get out of here." He snuggled up against my leg. "Thanks, Henry. You're such a good boy."

Although I was no longer faint, my thoughts were reeling at the speed of light. Leaving work before I'd found more volunteers made me nervous, but my brain was fried from worrying.

The office was quiet as I gathered my things and grabbed Henry's leash. My fatigue was so overwhelming it made the ten-minute walk to the parking lot feel impossible. As Henry and I slowly made our way to my car, it finally started to sink in that my struggles were not simply the result of an increased workload. My lousy health and addled brain were making everything worse.

When we reached the car, I could barely catch my breath. This was not the first time this kind of thing had happened, but it was definitely the worst.

Okay, I give up, I surrender. My doctors are right: I need to take some time off. Maybe I'm more run-down than I thought. Maybe I'll get stronger if I let myself rest. As soon as Henry and I got home I slipped into bed, but before I fell asleep, I felt his warm little body crawl under the covers and snuggle up next to me.

"It's okay, Henry. We're done for now." I fell into a resigned, peaceful slumber for twelve hours.

In the morning, I called Dr. Rose and told her I was in bad shape and ready to follow her orders to go on a medical leave from work.

"I really think you need to be hospitalized for malnutrition," she advised.

"I know, but I'm too scared. Hospitals feel like prisons. If I just stop working for a while, I think I'll get better," I said through my mildly diminished screen of denial.

"Well I can't force you, but I do recommend it. I'm happy to write a letter for your employer. I'm going to specify that you will be out for at least three months, at which time I will re-evaluate, but it really should be much longer."

"Thank you, Dr. Rose, I really appreciate your help," I said as we finished our conversation. I knew she was right about me needing to be hospitalized, but being away from my animals and Don would be too traumatic. Being able to admit that I was not strong enough to do my job was a big step for me and it gave me a huge sense of relief. I didn't know what the coming weeks or months would bring, but I knew anything would be better than pretending I was well enough to work.

***

My commitment to healing crystallized a few days later when I received a phone call from my brother John. Every couple of months he called, usually on a Saturday or Sunday morning when I was at work. He would cheerfully share what was going on with his happy family, which included his pretty and soft-spoken wife Tammy, his two pre-teen children Max and Bella, and their dog Lola. Of my three siblings John was the most conventional. His positive outlook and practical approach to life always comforted me, and when I got his phone call that

Saturday morning, I didn't expect to hear anything different.

"Hi, Marth. How's it going?"

"Hey, John! I'm okay, how about you?"

"I need to tell you what's been going on." His tone got serious, which made me hold my breath.

"I shared this with Mom a few months ago, but I wanted to tell the rest of you guys what's been going on."

"Okay," I said, feeling nervous, "What's up?"

"A year ago, I went to the doctor for a routine checkup and told him I'd been more tired than usual lately. I figured it was just because I was fifty years old, but the doctor ran a few blood tests that showed some abnormalities. Then he ran a few more that showed that I have multiple myeloma. That's bone marrow cancer." Silence.

"Oh God," was all I could say. My heart dropped into my stomach. Bone marrow cancer was a bad one, I was pretty sure, but John was calm. I wanted to burst into tears, but my better judgment told me to hold myself together and stay strong for him.

In his characteristically brave, unwavering style, he explained all the medical details of the diagnosis. He also shared that he would be undergoing many phases of treatment, including chemotherapy and stem cell transplant surgery. As bad as it sounded, he sounded optimistic.

My health concerns and recent need to stop working seemed minor and self-indulgent compared to John's news, but when I told him what was going on with me, he acknowledged the seriousness of it and offered his vote of confidence. I wanted to support John as much as he supported me, but that meant I would need to get stronger.

"We can cheer each other on as we get better," I said optimistically, wondering if people ever recovered from multiple myeloma.

"Yeah," he said with his usual confidence, "this cancer doesn't know who it's dealing with."

I envied John's courage, but more than that, I envied the fact that he had no shame about being sick, and knew without a doubt that he wanted to get well. My brain didn't work that way. The voices in my head were at odds. One of them wouldn't even acknowledge that I was sick, and insisted that I stop feeling sorry for myself. Another told me I was very sick and that it was a good thing because it meant I was getting closer to death, *and* it kept people from making demands on me. And another, healthier voice that had come into my head after hearing John's news told me I was sick and that like him, I could get better. Was it possible to turn up the volume on that one?

CHAPTER 20

Going Home

AFTER BEING AWAY FROM my job for several months, the stress in my life was significantly lower, but I still felt crappy. My weight was still very low, and I had no stamina. The healthy voice in my head encouraged me to go to Wisconsin to visit my mother. Two years had passed since I'd traveled home, because I'd been too anxious to take a vacation from work. I was afraid I wouldn't be able to catch up with my assignments when I returned. My "weekend" days were not even consecutive because the thought of dealing with piled-up phone messages and emails was too daunting. How did the rest of the world do it?

In the past, when I'd taken a few days off to go home to Wisconsin, I'd spent the whole time worrying and checking my emails, so I could never relax or fully enjoy my time with my mother. My unused vacation days piled up after several years and eventually I lost them, but I didn't care.

When I called my mother to ask if I could visit she was thrilled. And she assured me that Henry was welcome too. I needed him more than ever now.

On our day of departure, Henry and I got up at 4:00 a.m. to have a little breakfast before heading to the airport. Trudging through the airport would take energy, and I didn't want my blood sugar dropping. My willingness to eat a good breakfast on this first day of my journey surprised and pleased me. Starting off with a healthy mindset was a good sign.

Don graciously drove us to the airport at 5:00 a.m. There was no way I could have negotiated the freeways in my weakened state.

Henry had proven he was a good traveler when we'd flown to Mom's a few years earlier, so I was comfortable bringing him along. I would have loved to have taken Cassie and Dixie with me, but the logistics of that would have been challenging, if not impossible. Besides, they needed to keep Don company while I was away.

As a service dog, Henry was permitted to be out of his crate and on my lap on the plane, but on our previous trip, he had preferred to stay in his crate for much of the flight. During our layover in Detroit, he'd gotten out to stretch his little legs, and seemed totally content with that.

Twenty years earlier, when I was living in New York with Gus, I had taken him on flights when I went home to Mom's, but since he wasn't a service dog, he had to travel in a big crate in cargo. He was always a good sport and never seemed fazed by flying. When I was in my twenties and thirties, I loved flying, whether it was to Mom's or to some foreign country for adventure. It was always fun then, even on the long, international flights. However, things had changed, and on this trip home I had a very different experience.

Don dropped us off at LAX in the early morning light, and I checked my suitcase. Then Henry and I headed to the TSA line. Before attempting to go through the magnetic screening doorway I told the TSA agent that I couldn't remove my backpack because it was connected to me with a tube for my nutrition. He nodded, then got a female agent to assist me. She asked me to step behind a small curtain, then instructed me to remove my jacket and stand with my arms out like a "T." She explained that she was going to be touching me with the back of her hand, which she did, pretty much from head to toe, warning me every time she touched another body part. Next, she used little pieces of tape to "take samples" from my hands, the tube, pump, and backpack. She was very gracious and patient and went out of her way to make sure I knew what she was doing at every moment.

When finished with me, she asked if Henry would go with her through the screening doorway. He was okay with that, so they sent him through. No alarms went off.

The last thing Ms. TSA did was go through the contents of Henry's crate, which included a little fleece blanket and his favorite toy, Big Dog, a tri-color, stuffed dog that was nearly as big as he was. Henry stood patiently and watched Ms. TSA touch the little piece of test tape to Big Dog. Thankfully, he cleared TSA. What would Henry have done if they confiscated Big Dog? When Ms. TSA was finished she said I could pack up and go. The carefulness and respect with which all the TSA agents treated me during the fifteen-minute affair suggested that they were anticipating resistance or outrage from me. Maybe they'd dealt with people who had resisted or felt violated by their requests. I didn't feel that way at all. In fact, I felt special.

Once I got myself and Henry put back together, we found our gate. We waited until everyone else had boarded before we tried, because the crowds made me nervous. Henry's crate was cumbersome, and I wanted as much space as possible to carry him on. Besides, I knew they wouldn't take off without us. What was the hurry?

With Henry safely in his crate, I started my walk into the plane. My seat was near the back of the aircraft, and as I plodded toward it a crushing sensation came over my shoulders and chest, and I started to panic. *This plane is so small and there are so many people on board: we're going to run out of air! I better get off. Can I still get off? The door is shut. Damn! I'm not going to be able to breathe in here. If I beg the flight attendant maybe she'll let us get off . . .*

"Please take your seat, ma'am," the flight attendant directed me. Just then the man standing in front of my seat stepped aside so I could sit down. My heart was beating fast and hard and my head felt hot. I clutched Henry's crate tightly. Inside I could see his ears were on high alert as he watched me.

I opened the crate and brought Henry out onto my lap. Nudging his crate under the seat with my foot, I made room to stretch out my legs so he could settle on my lap. His eyes were wide open, staring into mine. *When did airplane seats get so small? Are all these other people uncomfortable? They're bigger than me. How do they fit?*

"Good boy, Henry." He started licking my face without a command, because he knew I was in trouble. He placed his front paws on my chest and licked me some more.

"Thank you, honey, good boy." I held him close. For the few minutes Henry was helping me, my heart slowed down and I felt less trapped. *Why are airlines making the seats smaller when people are getting bigger?* I couldn't imagine how uncomfortable it must be for the large man sitting next to me. *Didn't he feel squished and claustrophobic? Why wasn't he panicking?*

"Ma'am, you need to fasten your seatbelt for take-off," the cheerful flight attended instructed me.

"Yes, of course. Can my dog stay on my lap?"

"Is he a service dog?"

"Yes ma'am. Do you need to see his papers?" I scrambled to get them from my backpack, which was still on my back. "Just so you know, I can't put my pack in the overhead bin because I'm attached to it." I lifted up my shirt to show her that the enteral feeding tube was connected to a port on my chest.

"That's fine. Can you strap it in with you?" she asked.

"I think so," I said pulling the strap over my lap and backpack. "So it's okay for Henry to stay?"

"Yes, that's fine," she said very calmly. By this time my panic was subsiding, and with Henry's presence, I knew I would be okay. I closed my eyes, pulled Henry closer, and waited for the plane to take off.

As the plane accelerated and lifted off the runway, I sat motionless with my eyes closed. My breathing slowed, and once we were at cruising altitude, I pulled down the tray table in front of me. Above it was a little TV screen. That was cool. The big, colorful buttons told me I could choose a movie or a TV program. As I scrolled through the movie choices, I was happy to see that most of them were free. The film *Locke* got my attention. It was about a man played by Tom Hardy who was stuck in traffic. As he sat, he made a total of thirty-six phone calls to his work colleagues, his wife, and a woman with whom he had a one-night stand. One of his calls revealed that he was on his way to see the one-night-stand woman because she was about to give birth to his child.

Watching Tom Hardy's character attempt to orchestrate and explain his predicament to his workmates, his betrayed and heartbroken wife, and the emotionally fragile mother of his child was so engaging, I forgot about my suffocating surroundings. His character was trapped on so many levels that my situation paled in comparison.

After the movie, Henry and I slept until the plane landed in Detroit, where we boarded another plane for a one-hour flight to Appleton. Even though the plane was smaller than the first one, I didn't feel trapped or uncomfortable at all. Henry sensed the shift in my state of mind and relaxed as well. We took off, got to cruising altitude, and within ten minutes started our descent. Before I had time to get bored, we were on the ground. I'd never been so happy to be in Wisconsin.

CHAPTER 21

Lying Fallow

MY MOTHER LIVES IN a bustling community in eastern Wisconsin, but if you stand in her living room and look out the back window, it's easy to forget you're in a city. Just beyond the lush green lawn is a heavily wooded area with thick underbrush and tall trees. If you look past the trees, you'll see the Fox River, rapidly moving toward the dam, half a mile east. If you watch long enough, you may see a family of pelicans with white bodies, jet-black wings, and pouched orange bills diving for their dinner.

The road she lives on runs parallel to the river, so all the homes have backyards that slope into the valley. This intriguing urban forest is home to all sorts of animals including foxes, raccoons, deer, groundhogs, squirrels, chipmunks, hawks, and bald eagles. When my mother retired early from her job as a research chemist for a big paper corporation, she taught herself the art of photography, and over the years she has captured wonderful scenes in her back yard. My favorite photos are from a series she took of a mother fox with her five kits. By happy chance, the fox built her den and had her litter in the woods behind my mother's house, then brought them out each day for a month as she weaned them. Mom captured outstanding photos of the kits jumping and playing, and generally exhausting their poor mother.

The land in front of my mother's house is another natural wonderland. For decades, the seventy-nine-acre plot was a private, nine-hole golf course, which we were not allowed to play on when I was a kid. I obeyed the rules between May and September, when the presence of plaid-clad golfers kept me away, but as soon as the weather got cold or wet, I ran around to my heart's content on the lavish green fairways.

In recent years, this landmark golf course closed due to financial difficulties. That surprised me, because I never imagined that the wealthy people in town would stop golfing. Had all the members gotten too old to golf? Did the young wealthy people not play golf? Were country clubs a thing of the past? It saddened me to hear that this permanent fixture from my childhood no longer existed.

When Mom first told me that the club had gone belly up, I pictured the beautiful golf course falling into ruins. The image triggered my childhood fear of being abandoned, and living in rags on the street. That never would have happened, because my mother took such good care of us, but whenever I saw empty, old houses or vacant buildings, I got depressed.

Mom had told me that since my last visit, the land had been left to grow wild so the soil could lie fallow. It needed this time of wild growth to allow all the pesticides from years of being groomed as a golf course to come to the surface. After that, it would be safe for new growth. Hearing this made me apprehensive about seeing it. I would miss the lush, green fairways that for years were cared for so loyally.

Mom explained that after the ground was turned over and safe to use, the new, nonprofit owners started transforming it into a community garden. In addition to providing organic produce for the community, they offered an employment program for people coming out of rehab who needed to learn job skills. The new owners had also graciously opened up the garden so people could use it for walking and biking. That lifted my spirits.

When Henry and I got into the terminal, I spotted Mom immediately, because the Fox Cities airport is pleasantly small. We hugged, which was especially comforting, then I got my suitcase from the baggage carousel and we got in the car. Being back with my mother felt so good. As I sat in the passenger seat with Henry on my lap, I knew I was going to be okay.

We reached her house at 3:00 p.m., so there was still enough daylight to see what had become of the golf course. The once-perfect fairways were now prairies of long grass, and the formerly manicured greens had exploded into lively seas of bright yellow dandelion blooms. As soon as I put my suitcase in the house, I grabbed Henry and ran onto what used to be the sixth fairway.

Henry's little legs didn't allow him to see much as we walked through the deep grass, but he happily bounced along with me. Hawks and eagles soared overhead, searching for rodents that scurried deep in the long grass. Wild turkeys strutted around like they owned the place, and a pair of geese honked as they guarded their nest on the edge of the fairway. When Henry got a look at the huge turkeys, his ears went back and he stopped in his tracks. I encouraged him to walk with me so we could get a better look, but he dug in his heels. Evidently the turkeys were more dangerous than I thought. We decided to watch them from a distance.

Being surrounded by the thick, long grass and big trees put me in a dreamy state, and all that mattered was the present moment. Henry and I spent an hour exploring this enchanting new garden. For the rest of my weeklong visit at Mom's, we returned to the garden for at least an hour each day. We walked, meditated, and did yoga in the grass. The bleak images in my head of a forgotten golf course were replaced with visions of a lush, wild garden full of promise and hope.

When we weren't indulging in the garden, Henry and I sat with Mom and talked. This was the first time in more than three decades of visiting her that I didn't feel the need to be moving all the time. Nor was I compelled to check my phone and email every waking moment. Nope, on this visit, with Henry reminding me to eat and rest, I was at peace with myself and the world. Henry demonstrated on a daily basis that dogs live in this state all the time. Just looking at him reminded me to do the same. *Live in the moment. Enjoy this time with your mom.*

One evening the phone rang and Mom picked it up in the study.

"Hi, John!" I heard her say. I hurried in to join her. "How are you?" He must have said he was okay because she smiled. As I listened to her side of their conversation, I could tell they were making plans for John to come visit for a couple of days. He was still on medical leave after going through stem cell transplant surgery, so he had time to come see us.

"Are you sure you're strong enough to drive? We could come see you," Mom offered. John lived in Chicago, a three-hour drive from Appleton. "Okay, that's fine. We'll be here."

John arrived the next day to spend the weekend with us. When he got out of his car, I was shocked to see how thin he was. He was over six feet tall, and like everyone else in our family, had always been lean, but now he looked gaunt, and I felt sick to my stomach. In all the years I had been underweight, I had had no idea how my appearance made people feel, probably because I didn't see myself as thin, but seeing John's hollow cheeks and bony limbs covered by his baggy clothes made me think he was close to death.

"Hey, Marf," John said, using the nickname he had coined when I was a kid.

"Hey, John." We hugged each other. "How are you?"

"Not bad. I get tired fast, but that will get better."

"Let's sit down." Mom invited us. We headed into the kitchen. "Can I get you something to eat?"

"No thanks," John said. "My appetite has been lousy since my surgery." Hearing John say he had no appetite made me feel closer to him. We had something in common.

"How did everything go?" I asked, meaning the surgery.

"Two months ago, I had the stem-cell transplant, and before that I had three months of chemo."

"What was all that like?" I asked.

"For the transplant, they were able to use my cells, so I didn't need a donor."

"That's good."

"To start with, they gave me a medication to make body produce a kind of cells called hematopoietic stem cells."

"Sounds complicated."

"Before getting the stem cells, they gave me another high dose of chemo, which hopefully completely destroyed the bone marrow and wiped out as many of the cancer cells as possible. I thought of you because they put a big catheter in my chest to harvest the stem cells. You've had a few catheters in your time, right?"

"Still do." I pulled down the collar of my shirt to expose my Port-a-Cath. It was fun to share battle scars with John. It reminded me of when we would get scratched up as kids while building forts or climbing trees.

"Then I got Neupogen shots twice a day for five days. That's the drug that stimulates the production of the stem cells. It gave me throbbing bone pain, but that meant it was working. After the shots, they did the harvesting part, which was two days of hanging out hooked to the plasmapheresis machine. Fortunately, the harvest was successful, and they got enough cells to save if I needed them again in the future."

"Let's hope you won't need them."

"Then came the long-awaited transplant day. The nurse came in with a little IV bag of yellowish fluid, attached it to my catheter, and infused it for thirty minutes. When it was done, I thought, *That's it?* What a big anticlimax; some transplant. Hopefully all this 'rescued' the bone marrow and restored my immune system. Some people call it 'resetting the hard drive.'" He spoke optimistically, something I always admired about him.

"How's Tammy holding out through all this?" Mom asked.

"She's good. She really helped me through the next part, which I wasn't prepared for. The effects of the chemo started to kick in. I was really tired, had bad diarrhea, and mouth sores that made it hard to swallow. Fourteen days after that, the cells started to 'engraft,' meaning they were finding their way to the bone marrow and starting to function, but this was when the white blood cell count went down and my immune system was shot. That was the critical time. With no defenses, any type of infection could have been disastrous. Tammy and I had to stay in a special hospital hotel room, and Tammy had to wear a mask and make sure everything was sterilized when she made meals. My diarrhea and mouth sores went away, but I was still really fatigued."

"So, what happens next?"

"We just wait. They'll run blood tests every couple of months, but only time will tell."

"You are so brave," I told him. I'd always thought of him as a resilient person, but I was especially impressed by how well he was handling this.

John stayed for another day, and since we were both low-key, we mostly just talked. Although he was optimistic, he was also very practical, and told me he was in the process of making the necessary provisions for his wife and kids for when he died. The painful reality was that he may not live more than a couple years. He was too young to be making end-of-life decisions, but even as he spoke of his probable early demise, he didn't show any trace of self-pity. He believed he could get strong again and return to life as he knew it, but he also knew how important it was to allow enough time for that to happen. I needed to see that.

After John went back to Chicago, I resumed my precious one-on-one time with Mom. We spent a lot of time just talking at her kitchen table, which looked out onto the evolving wild garden. She listened as I processed all my feelings about my work situation. Sharing everything with her, good and bad, was easy because she didn't judge me. She responded by reminding me of my strengths.

In the evenings, we sat in her living room and looked out into the woods. On several occasions, we saw a family of deer, a doe and three fawns, looking around for their dinner. Mom loved seeing them and didn't mind that they ate her plants. When they got their fill, they gracefully wandered away. The deer were often followed by a big, chubby groundhog that waddled into the yard to find fresh vegetation.

One morning near the end of my stay, I woke after a solid night's sleep and had an epiphany. I quickly pulled on some clothes and went downstairs to find my mother. It was 7:30 a.m., and she'd been up for hours when Henry and I appeared.

"Good morning," she said and gave me a hug. "Hi, Henry." He wiggled his butt at her.

"Good morning." I hugged her back, then opened the front door so Henry could visit the bushes. I was excited to share my early morning insight with Mom. Henry did his business and came back in.

"There's some coffee here, but I can make you a stronger pot," she kindly offered.

"Thanks, this is fine," I said, pouring the weak coffee, which I truly preferred.

"Just let me know, and I'll make another pot. How did you sleep?" she asked.

"Great. I don't think I woke up once. That never happens at home. How'd you sleep?"

"Oh, pretty well," she said. I wanted to believe her, but I knew her back was bothering her. Years of untreated scoliosis had left her with a deformed, S-shaped spine and had reduced her height from 5'10" to 5'5". How strange it felt now to stand next to my once statuesque mother and see eye to eye. The "S" of her spine was compressing her body so her ribcage now rested on her hip bones, but she didn't complain.

"Being here with you has been so nice, Mom. Thank you for having me." *I have the best mom in the world.*

"You're always welcome. And so is Henry."

"Since I got here I've felt so peaceful, and I've been able to think things through. You know how anxious I've been about going back to work, right?"

"You don't think you're ready, do you?" She asked with concern.

"No, I don't. Just the opposite. When I woke up this morning, I had a realization. Before I started my leave of absence, I'd been dutifully going to work expecting my strength to magically reappear. I kept thinking that if I just pushed myself hard enough, my stamina would return, but it hasn't. Even when I reduced my schedule to part-time, I felt worn out all the time. I'd get overwhelmed and feel faint within a couple of hours. Now that I've been away from that environment, I can see how unhealthy my efforts were. After seeing how John is allowing himself to heal, I finally understand that I haven't given myself a chance to get better.

"My body is like the golf course and needs to lie fallow before it can come back to life. I'm hoping that if I let myself be dormant for a while, maybe I can 'grow back' in a healthier state. And hopefully, at some point I'll be able to give back to the world again, like the garden."

"That all sounds sensible. So what are you going to do?"

"I think extending my medical leave would just postpone the inevitable. Dr. Rose was right: the best thing for me to do is to resign completely. That way I won't feel guilty about stringing my boss along, and I'll have a chance to actually get better."

"Let me know what I can do to help," Mom offered.

"You've already helped me so much. Getting my batteries recharged here with you has sparked my hope and cleared my head so I can see what I need to do next. I have to just trust that everything will be okay."

"I'm sure you'll be fine."

"I'm going to email my letter of resignation to Erin today. Then she can move forward and hire someone else, and I can stop worrying about it."

"She may not be surprised." Mom was right. Erin probably wouldn't be surprised at all. She had seen me unraveling for months.

"I'm going to miss the people, especially Erin, but I won't miss the work anymore." At that moment, Henry approached me and put his little feet on my legs, as though he needed to Lap Up.

"Sweet Henry, come on up." I lifted him up and he licked my face. "This little guy will really miss the zoo. He loves going to work. I wouldn't have survived the last few months without him."

"He's very sensitive to your needs," Mom observed.

"You know, it's funny, because originally I got Henry thinking he'd make it possible for me to keep working. He's definitely helped me over the years, and he's gotten me through a lot, but now I see that he's done something even bigger than that for me."

"What do you mean?" Mom was curious.

"If it weren't for Henry, I don't think I would have ever realized that I need to totally stop working. I'd still be beating my head against the wall trying. I'm a little stubborn, as you may have noticed."

"I'm glad you have Henry to help you."

"You're so good to me. Thank you, Mom. This is the first time in my life I'm not scared of what the future holds. In fact, I'm kind of excited about it. I feel free for the first time."

"You'll be able to spend more time writing," Mom reminded me. "I know you enjoy that." She was right. Henry had been a big inspiration for me to write, and I had several book ideas brewing in my head.

"I'm definitely looking forward to that. And Henry can help me, can't you, buddy?" I smooched the top of his head. "I'm sorry we have to go back to LA tomorrow. We've both really enjoyed being here with you."

"I've enjoyed having you both. You're welcome anytime."

"Thanks Mom. I love you."

"I love you too, honey."

***

Saying goodbye to Mom was hard because I felt so safe with her. As I sat on the plane back to Los Angeles, I trusted that everything was going to be okay. Henry, who was curled up on my lap, would encourage me to try harder to take care of myself. If I had any willingness to heal, his love would ground me and remind me that life was worth living. His conviction and dedication never faltered. Watching him eat and play reminded me that these behaviors were necessary and normal, not optional. Even when he was not performing a specific command, his shiny black eyes and snuggly warm body had the power to keep me emotionally and spiritually conscious.

When I adopted Henry and chose to get him trained, I did myself a great favor. Going through the certification process and learning the pros and cons of having a service dog, especially a very small one, was not easy, but it was well worth the effort. Without him I wouldn't have been able to face reality or make necessary lifestyle changes. I wouldn't have been able to enter the next phase of my life.

THE END

Acknowledgments

I would like to thank the people at Koehler Books for their efforts: John Koehler, Joe Coccaro, Dana Salerno and of course, all the behind-the-scenes people with whom I have not had the pleasure to speak.

I also want to thank my mom for believing in me; my husband Don for supporting my dreams to write; and my service dog Henry for being there.

Bibliography

International Association of Assistance Dog Partners. www.iaadp.org/.

Kronkosky Charitable Foundation. www.kronkosky.org/research/Research_Briefs/Animal.

Gorman, Anna. "Mental-health advocate is also a symbol of recovery." *The Los Angeles Times,* July 30, 2012. articles.latimes.com/2012/jul/30/local/la-me-0730-mentalhealth-advocate-20120730.

Maeve: Psychiatric Service Dog and Mental Health Advocate. www.servicepoodle.com/.

The National Institutes of Health, News in Health. www.nih.gov.

Serpell, James. "Animal Companions and Human Well-Being: An Historical Exploration of the Value of Human-Animal Relationships," *Handbook on Animal-Assisted Therapy: Theoretical Foundations and Guidelines for Practice.* 2010.

Service Dog Central. www.servicedogcentral.org.

The U.S. Department of Justice, Civil Rights Division. Disability Right Section. www.ada.gov/regs2010/service_animal_qa.html#exc, www.ada.gov/service_animals_2010.htm.

Dreazen, Yochi J. "'Sit! Stay! Snuggle!': An Iraq Vet Finds His Dog Tuesday." *The Wall Street Journal,* July 11, 2009. www.wsj.com/articles/SB124727385749826169.

Resources

ANIMAL THERAPY

Animal Assisted Therapy—Animal Assisted Therapy Services - www.aatsct.org

Equine Assisted Therapy—eatherapy.org

Equestrian Therapy—www.equestriantherapy.com/types-of-equine-therapy

Therapet—www.therapet.org/about-us/what-is-animal-assisted-therapy

SERVICE DOGS

Pet Partners—petpartners.org/about-us

American Dog Trainers Network—inch.com/~dogs/service

Dog Capes—dogcapes.com

Certification Council for Pet Dog Trainers—www.ccpdt.org

Karen Pryor Academy—www.karenpryoracademy.com/find-a-trainer

Association of Pet Dog Trainers—apdt.com/resource-center

INVISIBLE DISABILITIES

Invisible Disabilities Association—invisibledisabilities.org/what-is-an-invisible-disability

IDA Facebook page—www.facebook.com/InvisibleDisabilities

Disabled World—www.disabled-world.com/disability/types/invisible

ANOREXIA NERVOSA

Mayo Clinic—www.mayoclinic.org/diseases-conditions/anorexia/home

National Eating Disorders Association—www.nationaleatingdisorders.org/anorexia-nervosa

The Bella Vita—www.thebellavita.com/signs-of-anorexia-html

WebMD—www.webmd.com/mental-health/eating-disorders/anorexia-nervosa/anorexia-nervosa-other-places-to-get-help

DEPRESSION AND BIPOLAR DISORDER

Depression and Bipolar Support Alliance—www.dbsalliance.org

Families for Depression Awareness—www.familyaware.org

Mayo Clinic—www.mayoclinic.com

National Institute of Mental Health—www.nimh.nih.gov

National Mental Health Information Center—www.samsha.gov

CROHN'S AND COLITIS

National Institutes of Health—www.niddk.nih.gov/health-information/digestive-diseases/microscopic-colitis

CrohnsandColitis.com—www.crohnsandcolitis.com

Crohn's and Colitis Foundation—www.crohnscolitisfoundation.org

WebMD—www.webmd.com/ibd-crohns-disease/ulcerative-colitis/microscopic-colitis

PRIMARY IMMUNE DEFICIENCY DISEASES

National Institutes of Health—ghr.nlm.nih.gov/condition/common-variable-immune-deficiency

Immune Deficiency Foundation—primaryimmune.org

IG Living—www.igliving.com/resources/ig-disorder-common-variable-immunodeficiency-cvid.html

ImmuneDisease.com—www.immunedisease.com/about-pi/types-of-pi/common-variable-immunodeficiency-cvid.html

National Organization of Rare Diseases—rarediseases.org/rare-diseases/common-variable-immune-deficiency

LIVING WITH A FEEDING TUBE

Summit Medical Group Library—www.summitmedicalgroup.com/library/adult_health/sha_tube_feeding

Feeding Tube Awareness Foundation—www.feedingtubeawareness.org, www.feedingtubeawarenessweek.org

The Oley Foundation—oley.org

Notes

(ENDNOTES)

1   http://www.ada.gov/regs2010/service_animal_
    qa.html#exc

2   http://www.iaadp.gov/service_animals_2010.htm

3   http://www.servicedogcentral.org

4   http:// www.servicedogcentral.org

5   http://www.servicepoodle.org

6   http://www.iaadp.org/

7   http://www.iaadp.org/psd_tasks.html

8   http://www.iaadp.org/psd_tasks.html

9   *The Wall Street Journal.* July 11, 2009. "Sit! Stay!
    Snuggle!" An Iraq Vet Finds His Dog Tuesday."

10 http://newsinhealth.nih.gov/2009/February/feature1.
    htm Can Pets Keep You Healthy?: Exploring the Human-
    Animal Bond.

11 NIH study.

12 NIH study.

13 NIH study.

14 Serpell, James "Animal Companions and Human Well-Being: An Historical Exploration of the Value of Human-Animal Relationships," *Handbook on Animal-Assisted Therapy: Theoretical Foundations and Guidelines for Practice*: pp.3-17.

15 Ibid.

16 http://www.kronkosky.org/research/Research_Briefs/ Animal TherapySept2008.pdfResearch Brief, "Animal Assisted Therapy," September 2008, The Kronkosky Charitable Foundation.

17 "A Voice Above the Rest," *Los Angeles Times*, July 30, 2012, by Anna Gorman.

CPSIA information can be obtained
at www.ICGtesting.com
Printed in the USA
FSOW03n0901031017
39446FS